Return Patterns of German Open-End Real Estate Funds

Corporate Finance and Governance

Herausgegeben von Dirk Schiereck

Band 1

PETER LANG

Frankfurt am Main · Berlin · Bern · Bruxelles · New York · Oxford · Wien

Sebastian Michael Gläsner

Return Patterns of German Open-End Real Estate Funds

An Empirical Explanation of Smooth Fund Returns

PETER LANG
Internationaler Verlag der Wissenschaften

Bibliographic Information published by the Deutsche Nationalbibliothek
The Deutsche Nationalbibliothek lists this publication in the Deutsche Nationalbibliografie; detailed bibliographic data is available in the internet at http://dnb.d-nb.de.

Zugl.: European Business School, Univ., Diss., 2009

Cover design:
Olaf Glöckler, Atelier Platen, Friedberg

D 1540
ISSN 1869-537X
ISBN 978-3-631-60406-9

www.peterlang.de

Geleitwort

Die politischen Entscheidungsträger in Deutschland übertragen die Verantwortung für die langfristige Alterssicherung mehr und mehr in die Hände eines jeden Einzelnen, der damit selbst an den Aktien-, Anleihe und Immobilienmärkten agieren soll (bzw. muss). Ein derartiger Risikotransfer, so sollte man meinen, geschehe vor dem Hintergrund einer fundierten Analyse der historischen Entwicklung der deutschen Kapital- und Investmentfondsmärkte mit allen Risiken und Renditeperspektiven. Da könnte es fast überraschen, dass es eine derartige Analyse zumindest für die drittbedeutendste Anlageklasse der Immobilienfonds bislang gar nicht gibt

Auch hier setzt die Dissertationsschrift von Herrn Gläsner an, wenn er uns auf der Basis einer sehr umfangreichen, einmaligen Datensammlung die langfristige Performance von deutschen offenen Immobilienfonds unter expliziter Berücksichtigung des sogenannten Survivorship Bias analysiert. Dieser Bias erfasst Verzerrungen in den Aussagen langfristig ausgelegter empirischer Analysen, die durch die fehlende Berücksichtigung des zwischenzeitlichen Ausscheidens vorwiegend schwach rentierlicher Fonds entstehen. Auf der Grundlage aller deutschen offenen Immobilienfonds, die in den letzten zwanzig Jahren irgendwann einmal in Deutschland aufgelegt waren, werden Zusammenhänge zwischen Performance, Bewertungsansätzen und saisonalen Effekten dokumentiert. Die Erkenntnisse dieser Auswertungen beschreiben zum einen ein bedeutsames Stück deutscher Nachkriegsgeschichte und tragen zum anderen hoffentlich zukünftig zu einer Verbesserung von Effizienz und Rentabilität bei der Strukturierung insbesondere von Privatanlegerportfolios bei und verbessern damit auch die langfristige Vermögensposition dieser Anleger.

Herr Gläsner verzichtet in seiner Arbeit weitestgehend auf eine politische Wertung seiner Ergebnisse. Diese Zurückhaltung mag für eine betriebswirtschaftliche Dissertationsschrift angemessen sein. Nichtsdestotrotz sollten gerade auch die wirtschaftspolitischen Entscheidungsträger in unserem Land diese Arbeit mit großer Aufmerksamkeit lesen. Sie enthält eine Fülle hoch interessanter Resultate zum Verständnis der zu erwartenden zukünftigen Performance von deutschen Immobilienanlagen und ist so geschrieben, dass es den Lesern sicherlich Freude machen wird, sie umfassend zu studieren. Ich wünsche der Arbeit und ihren Erkenntnissen eine weite Verbreitung.

Professor Dr. Dirk Schiereck

Danksagung

Viele Personen haben in erheblichem Umfang zum Gelingen der vorliegenden Doktorarbeit beigetragen, Ihnen gebührt mein herzlicher Dank.

An erster Stelle ist hier mein Doktorvater Dirk Schiereck zu nennen, der durch seine bedingungslose Unterstützung zu allen Zeiten die erfolgreiche Fortführung des Dissertationsprojektes ermöglicht hat. Meinem zweiten fachlichen Betreuer und Mitautor einiger Paper Matthias Thomas danke ich für zahlreiche stets konstruktive, anregende und lebhafte Diskussionen. Nicht zu letzt durch seine Einschätzungen und kritischen Einwände haben die kontroversen Arbeitsergebnisse erheblich an Belastbarkeit gewonnen.

Neben natürlichen Personen haben auch einige Institutionen einen wichtigen Anteil an der Arbeit: Mein Arbeitgeber, die Investment Property Databank GmbH, die während der gesamten Promotion einen sehr forschungsfreundlichen Rahmen geboten hat. Der Gesellschaft für Immobilienwissenschaftliche Forschung e.V. gilt mein Dank für die Organisation von Doktorandenkolloquien, Unterstützung zu Forschungskonferenzen und einen Zuschuss zu den Druckkosten der Arbeit. Dem Bundesverband Investment und Asset Management e.V. danke ich für die Nutzung des Archives. Dem Gesetzgeber danke ich für die Novellierung des Investmentgesetzes, die es erst ermöglichte, die Werte der einzelnen Immobilien der Immobilienfonds zu ermitteln.

Zurück zu den natürlichen Personen: Hier bedanke ich mich bei dem gesamten Team des Real Estate Management Institutes für die Unterstützung vom ersten „Office Day“ bis zur Disputation. Ich danke im Besonderen meinen langjährigen Doktoranden-Kollegen Fabian Brämisch für seinen mitreißenden Forschungselan, Hendrik Koch für nachhaltige Diskussionsabende und Felix Zeidler sowie Timo Schläfer für ihre Erfahrungen aus der Welt des Investmentbankings. Björn-Martin Kurzrock danke ich für eine Vielzahl von Ideen und Diskussionen, die wir in gemeinsamen Projekten umsetzen konnten. Bei Friederike Sperl bedanke ich mich für leidenschaftliche Diskussionen, die oftmals den Themenkreis von effizienten Märkten und anreizkompatiblen Vergütungssystemen gesprengt haben.

Meiner Familie gilt mein Dank für die uneingeschränkte Unterstützung auf allen Wegen. Ohne sie hätte sich Gegenwind eher rau als erfrischend angefühlt.

Sebastian Gläsner

Table of Contents

List of Tables

List of Figures

List of Abbreviations

ANOVA	Analysis of Variance
BVI	Bundesverband Investment und Asset Management e.V.
CREF	Commingled Real Estate Fund
DCF	Discounted Cash Flow
DIX	Deutscher Immobilien Index [German property index]
ERES	European Real Estate Society
EURIBOR	European InterBank Offered Rate
FV	Fund Volume
GAV	Gross Asset Value
GOEF	German Open-end Real Estate Fund
HHI	Herfindahl-Hirschman Index
INREV	European Association for Investors in Non-listed Real Estate Funds
IPD	Investment Property Databank
IPG GmbH	Investment Property Databank GmbH
N	Number of Observations
NA	Not Available
NAV	Net Asset Value
NCREIF	National Council of Real Estate Investment Fiduciaries
NPI	NCREIF Property Index
OFIX-ALL	Offene Fonds Immobilien Index [Open-end property fund index]
OFIX-10	Offene Fonds Immobilien Index [Open-end property fund index] with only those GOEFs that have at least ten years of return history
OLS	Ordinary Least Squares
REIT	Real Estate Investment Trust
REXP	Deutscher Rentenindex [German governmental bond index]
SW	Shapiro-Wilk
WC	Wilcoxon
WertV	Wertermittlungsverordnung [Appraisal act]

List of Symbols

$DERV_t$	Delta estimated rental value in period t
DMV_t	Delta market value in period t
$DOCR_t$	Delta occupancy rate in period t
DYP_t	Delta year's purchase in period t
MV_t	Market value in period t
OCR_t	Occupancy rate in period t
$occupancy.rate$	Occupancy rate
$perc.ending.leases$	Percentage of ending leases by rental value within the next year
R_t	Return in month t
RVG	Rental value growth
V_t^*	Value of property at time t
$year.of.purchase$	Year of the acquisition of the property by the fund
YP	Year's purchase or rent multiplier
a_2Feb	Dummy variable taking the value of 1 for the month February
$a_{12}Dec$	Dummy variable taking the value of 1 for the month December
ε	Random error term
τ	Quantile of the quantile regression function

1 Introduction and Overview

1.1 Introduction

German open-end retail funds (GOEF) represent the prevailing form of indirect real estate investment for private investors in Germany. By the end of 2008 44 funds have property investments of 90.0 bn. EUR under management. As funds employ financial leverage, gross asset values (GAV) exceed net asset values (NAV). In terms of net asset value of managed funds, only bond funds with 143.4 bn. EUR and equity funds with 133.6 bn. EUR rank before GOEFs with 84.3 bn. EUR NAV (BVI, 2009a).

Although funds are not listed at the stock market, the investment is highly liquid as participations can be redeemed to the investment company on a daily basis at NAV. This liquidity transformation from a daily available investment into long-term property allocation is a central characteristic of the investment product. To guarantee product liquidity and to protect the retail investor, funds are strictly regulated under the Investment Act (2008). The act comprises several regulations to limit the risk of a liquidity shortage. Funds have to hold at least 5% of gross asset value in cash, up to a maximum of 49%. The maximum leverage is also restricted to 50% of real estate asset value. In case of a liquidity squeeze however, funds are allowed to delay the redemption of participations up to twelve months[1], to protect remaining investors from a disadvantageous forced sale of properties. The Investment Act further more requires that every property is being appraised by an independent external appraiser at least once a year, on a rolling basis to distribute property value changes evenly over the year.

Internationally, non-listed open-end real estate funds have been much less successful than in Germany. Bannier, Fecht, and Tyrell (2008) compare the development of open-end funds globally. They conclude that the success over the last 50 years of GOEF was an internationally exception and they relate it to the institutional design and the German banking structure. Besides the daily availability of the investment, stable fund returns are a major argument for investors. Before the year 2008[2], no single fund showed a negative nominal return on a yearly basis over the last 50 years since the inception of the first GOEF.

The remarkably stable returns over time and property cycles have been examined by research for smoothing and lagging effects due to property valuation. The four presented essays of this dissertation contribute to the explanation of stable fund returns and smooth value changes of fund properties. The first two essays deal with value changes on the property level. Essay one (chapter 2) focuses on German properties of GOEF and compares value changes by portfolio

1 This period can be extended up to 24 months, if this extension is stipulated in the fund statutes (§ 81 Investment Act, 2008).

2 Ironically, the firstly initiated GOEF, EURO ImmoProfil, yields minus 3.4% in 2008 and breaks the tradition of positive GOEF returns.

in fund crisis year 2006. Essay two (chapter 3) compares value changes of foreign properties of GOEF and compares them to the capital growth of properties in domestic portfolios. Essay three (chapter 4) links developments on the property level (gross asset value) to the implications on the fund return level (net asset value). It relates property value changes within one reporting year to monthly fund return deviations. Essay four (chapter 5) builds on the results of essays one to three regarding smoothing effects on the property level and on the fund level. Calling into question frequently stated assumptions about the origin of autocorrelation within mutual real estate fund returns, the essay finds that calendar anomalies in fund returns contribute to the explanation of autocorrelation in returns.

The research objective firstly is to better understand stable capital growth of German properties and secondly to contribute to the explanation of stable GOEF returns. In the course of the investigation, evidence is found that both phenomena are interrelated. The relation from stable property capital growth rates to stable property fund returns is intuitively convincing, but empirical evidence weakens the validity of the relation (essay 3). A relation from stable fund returns (or return requirements) to stable property value changes seems not reasonable provided the fact the independent external valuers define property values and thus property value changes. However, empirical evidence suggests that this relation may hold nevertheless (essay 1 and 2). All analyses are based on publicly available data. The drawback of this approach is that in some cases the level of detail is limited in comparison to private information. The advantage of data non-confidentiality however offsets this drawback by far, as analyses are not limited by any kinds of client interests.

Research implications are comprehensive, both for research and practise. For research, evidence on consciously smoothed returns calls for different approaches to evaluate real estate investment risk. For practise, evidence on consciously smoothed returns has to be evaluated with respect to investor protection. Finally, evidence on client influence from fund management on valuers questions the independence of appraisers in the valuation context.

1.2 Essay 1: Research question and main findings

The essay analyses changes in market values of German properties of open-end funds in the year of the fund liquidity crisis 2006. Funds used foreign capital influx and compressed yields to sell off a big proportion of their German properties. In a highly liquid transaction market, market analysts described property prizes to be extremely rising, while the German properties of open-end funds on average lost in market value. Using publicly available data, analysis is not restricted by any confidentiality aspects. Results show large differences in value changes of properties between funds' portfolios in fund crisis year 2006. The findings question the accuracy of market values prior to 2006 for many portfolios and present evidence on client influence on appraisals. The level of the vacancy rate is significantly related to massive devaluations in 2006. As some portfolios show much lower dispersions of property value changes than others, estimation of idiosyncratic property risk relying on property indices is questioned. Market values of German open-end fund properties are analysed for the first time on an individual asset level and the results suggest serious valuation bias.

1.3 Essay 2: Research question and main findings

To the 31-12-2008, German open-end funds hold only 29.9% of their property investments in Germany. European markets without Germany account for 58.1% of property market values and 11.9% are invested outside Europe. The biggest individual markets outside Germany are France with 19.0% and the UK with 9.9% investment volume (BVI, 2009a). Intriguing is the contrast between the stable fund performances in times of worldwide financial turmoil and the developments on the mayor property markets the funds are invested in. The question arises why capital weighted returns of GOEFs (OFIX-ALL) that are invested to about 30% over all funds in France and the UK have experienced hardly any return variations within the years of booming property markets (2005-2007) and bearish property markets (2007-2009)?

As GOEFs are obliged by the Investment Act (2008) to publish market values of individual properties, the essay uses a dataset of 879 property values derived by external independent appraisal experts within the years 2004 to 2008. Valuations of properties held by GOEFs in Belgium, France, Italy, the Netherlands, Spain and the United Kingdom are compared to mean valuation figures reported by the Investment Property Databank (IPD) for the respective markets. Results show significant differences with respect to changes in market values for all countries in almost all analysed years. With respect to the rental values however, findings are ambiguous. The most extreme valuation differences between GOEFs and the IPD data are found for the UK and France.

1.4 Essay 3: Research question and main findings

Fund returns of GOEFs are very stable and have been examined by researchers for smoothing and lagging effects due to property valuation. Previous studies have found that fund returns show serial correlation on the index level and have unsmoothed returns to account for assumed appraisal smoothing effects. The essay analyses value changes on the individual property level and builds a link to monthly fund returns. Publicly available information on market values on the individual property level has been collected and can be analyzed without consideration of any confidentiality aspects, which makes it possible to account for portfolio differences. Results indicate significant effects of the timing of property valuations on the volatility of monthly fund returns. On a monthly basis, the link of property performance and fund returns is missing. Serial correlation of fund returns at twelve months time lag is found only for six out of twelve funds. The fact that half of the sample does not exhibit significant coefficients of serial correlation and the missing influence of individual property value changes on fund returns question the frequently stated assumption of autocorrelation caused by appraisal smoothing.

1.5 Essay 4: Research question and main findings

It has been shown that GOEFs fund returns are smoothed due to the timing of valuations (chapter 4). With respect to their German properties, there is evidence that the majority of funds did influence property appraisals in such a way that the strong yield compression in 2006 and 2007 was not reflected in value gains (chapter 2). All three essays find smoothing effects within GOEFs, either on portfolio level (chapter 4) or on individual property level (chapter 2 and 3). The investigation deepens into the issue of autocorrelation of fund returns and presents evidence that at least a big proportion of observed serial correlation of GOEF returns does not stem from the valuation process on the property level, but is rather due to calendar anomalies of fund returns. The results contribute to previous research on autocorrelation of fund returns in that respective that autocorrelation is examined on individual fund level as contrasted to autocorrelation on aggregated index level.

2 Appraisal within open-end real estate funds: Evidence on biased appraisals in fund crisis year 2006

2.1 *Introduction*

German property markets experienced in 2006 and 2007 an unprecedented yield compression. Market analysts like AtisReal, BulwienGesa, CBRE and DEGI reported a decline of yields in all mayor German office markets due to high capital inflows by foreign investors (Figure 2.1).

The unweighted average office prime yield of the German top five office markets Berlin, Düsseldorf, Frankfurt, Hamburg and Munich declined by more than 60 basis points between 2004 and 2007. For the year 2006, the strongest yield compression is reported.

Figure 2.1 Prime office yields of the top 5 German office markets 2004-2007

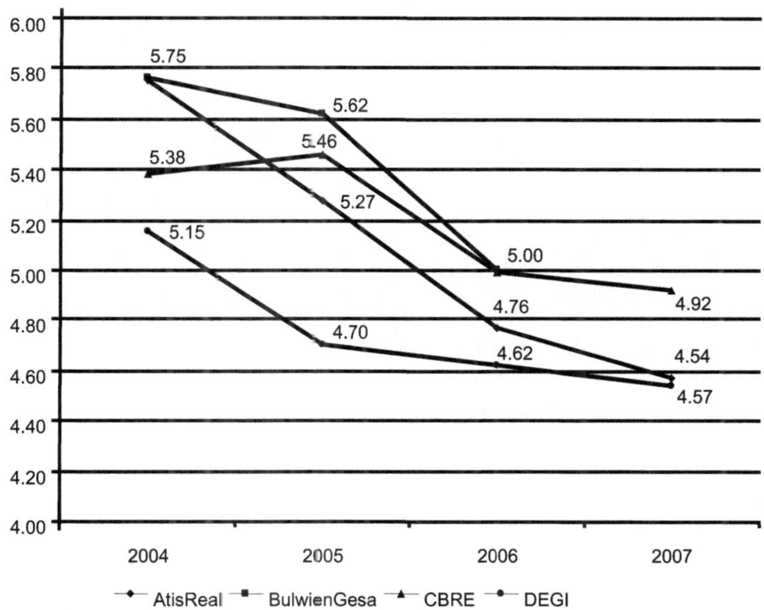

The figure shows average (not capital weighted) prime yields of the top 5 German office locations Berlin, Düsseldorf, Frankfurt, Hamburg and Munich as reported by major real estate consultants.

Analogue to the rise in demand and the decline in yields, market participants agree that property values in Germany in the years 2006 and 2007 rose significantly (Crosby, 2007).

At the same time, the beginning of 2006 demarks a severe crisis for the German open-end fund industry, because for the first time in the 50-year history, three out of 24 funds[3] had to stop the redemption of participations.

Funds state in their accounts that they used the extraordinary good market conditions in 2006 and 2007 to sell off German properties in an unprecedented amount. A study on German open-end real estate retail funds reports that funds decreased their portfolio share of German properties from 41.0% of property values in 2006 to 31.5% in 2007 (IPD 2008, p. 28). In absolute terms this equals net sales of German properties in 2006 of 6.7 bn. EUR and 2.8 bn. EUR in 2007. The capital growth of all German properties of the German property index DIX in 2006 was negative with -3.6% in 2006 and turned positive in 2007 with 2.1% (IPD 2008, p. 19). The data published by IPD as a result of the valuations and transaction proceeds of German properties for the year 2006 is in sharp contrast to the market description of real estate agents and consultants mentioned before, despite the fact that market liquidity and the availability of transaction comparables were very high at this time.

This leads to the question why in times of booming property markets the values of German open-end retail funds' properties decline? The paper addresses this question by analyzing all value changes of the standing investments of German open-end real estate retail funds between 2004 and 2007. Unfortunately, not all funds published property values on the individual level before 2006 and thus the analysis of the years 2005 and 2006 is restricted to the funds that did so already. The presumptive evidence stated so far rises questions regarding valuation accuracy (see also literature review). The paper seeks to understand more about valuation practice on the portfolio level by applying an analysis of variance to see whether there is a link between the ownership of a property to a particular fund and its valuation in crisis year 2006.

2.2 Literature review

When appraisals of comparable properties differ on portfolio level, a frequently stated assumption is that clients have influenced appraisers. Therefore, the first part of the literature review analyses whether it is possible and seems to be likely that appraisers were influenced by fund management. The second part addresses the consequences of biased appraisals for return measurement on the portfolio level.

---

3 The total number of open-end real estate funds regulated by the German Investment Act (2008) was 43 by end 2005, but only 24 of them are open to retail investors.

2.2.1 Fund management influence on appraisers

A similar study in the context of the presented paper has been presented as a working paper just recently by Crosby et al. at the European Real Estate Society (ERES) conference 2009. They investigate whether open-end funds' management in the UK influenced appraisers in the market downturn of 2007 to adjust values downwards more quickly. Crosby et al. (2009b) present a comprehensive review of client motivation to influence appraisers, possible means to exert influence and market circumstances in that influence seems more likely to occur. They argue that in the time of rapid property value decline in the UK in the second half of 2007, open-end funds in contrast to other market participants had a strong incentive to have their properties quickly marked down to market. They mention in this context that some fund managers switched to a fortnightly valuation frequency to ensure that capital redemptions were met at the current market value. The valuers on the other side were faced with much higher uncertainty for their appraisal values since the transaction volumes fell markedly. To empirically test their hypothesis, they use the IPD UK database and brake down quarterly performance data by fund type and find that the falls in capital values for open-end funds were significantly greater than for the remaining fund types and that the differences being most marked in the first half of 2007.

With respect to the German property market, so far there exists no research that compares property performance differentiated by investor type[4]. Besides this, no research exists on client influence on valuation, which internationally is a major research topic (Table 2.1). The majority of studies examine the US and the UK market, while in recent times New Zealand, Nigeria and Taiwan / Singapore gained more attention. Due to confidentiality issues, most studies have an experimental setting, either theory building, with usually small sample sizes and in-depth interviews, or theory testing, with usually larger surveys. Almost all studies within the commercial sector find evidence on client influence on valuation, with respect to the residential market results are less clear.

The absence of research on client influence on valuation in Germany is particularly problematic as the main participants[5] on the German commercial property market, namely the open-end funds, comprise many characteristics that are prone to result in client influence. Building on a model developed by Levy and Schuck (2005), Table 2.2 shows the factors that are most relevant for client influence and evaluates the parameter values of GOEFs. The factors are directly taken from Levy and Schuck (2005, p. 196).

---

4 On fund level, Kurzrock, Gläsner, and Wilke (2009) compare returns of German open-end real estate retail funds with open-end specialist funds. Due to data limitations, the investigation does not address performance on the property level.

5 By the end of 2008, GOEFs account for 40.0% of property values within the IPD Germany database and form the biggest group of market participants (IPD GmbH, 2009a). Closed-end funds and foreign investors are also major market participants, but they usually do not report data to IPD.

Table 2.1 Research on client influence on valuation

Author	Theory	Data	Property type	Country	Client influence?
Diaz (1990)	building	experiment	res.	US	yes
Diaz et al. (2002)	building	experiment	com.	UK,NZ	
Levy & Schuck (1999)	building	experiment	com.	NZ	yes
Levy & Schuck (2005)	building	experiment	com.	NZ	yes
Rushmore (1993)	building	theoretical	com.		yes
Smith (1986)	building	theoretical	com.		
Smolen (1994)	building	theoretical	com.		yes
Amidu & Aluko (2007)	testing	experiment	com.	NI	yes
Amidu, Aluko, & Hansz (2008)	testing	experiment	com.	NI	yes
Chen & Yu (2009)	testing	experiment	com.	TW,SI	yes
Cypher & Hansz (2003)	testing	experiment	com.	US	yes
Diaz & Hansz (2001)	testing	experiment	com.	US	yes
Diaz (1997)	testing	experiment	com.	US	
Gallimore & Wolverton (2000)	testing	experiment	com.	UK	yes
Havard (1999)	testing	experiment	ind.	UK	yes
Havard (2001)	testing	experiment	ind.	UK	yes
Kinnard et al. (1997)	testing	experiment	com.	US	yes
Smolen & Hambleton (1997)	testing	experiment	com.	US	yes
Spence & Thorson (1998)	testing	experiment	res.	US	
Wolverton & Gallimore (1999)	testing	experiment	com.	US	yes
Wolverton (2000)	testing	experiment	com.	US	yes
Worzala et al. (1998)	testing	experiment	res.	US	yes
Firoozi et al. (2006)	testing	private	res.	US	yes
Ferguson (1988)	testing	private	com.	US	yes

With respect to **client characteristics**, GOEFs can be considered to strongly influence valuers in three out of four factors. They are *big* and *sophisticated clients* with a close *relationship to the valuers*. For the factor *type of client* a classification is not possible, as no prior research on GOEF client influence exists. For the **external characteristics**, the *definition of market value* has to be considered weakly defined, considering for example the idea of "sustainable" rental values (see e.g. Downie et al., 1996), which results in a strong potential influence on valuers. For the remaining two factors *regulatory framework* and *market conditions* of the valuation industry there are no clear differences to e.g. the situation in the UK, although the valuation industry in Germany seems to be more diversified. The **valuation characteristics** show most clearly that GOEFs are to be classified as potentially influencing valuers. For all four factors, the characteristics of GOEFs are likely to result in a strong influence on valuations. The *range of defensible values* is high, as the example of Deka-ImmobilienFonds in 2006 clearly proves. In a German property market surrounding of strong yield compression and rather stable capital values of the properties of the other GOEFs, the Deka-ImmobilienFonds portfolio comprising 129 German properties was devalued by -18.8%[6]. The *amount of opinion* involved in the appraisal of complex commercial properties is high, and the *valuation result* is highly important for fund management. A stable return development is crucial for the asset class of GOEFs, as return stability was the major sales argument over the last 50 years since inception of the first fund, and the fragile capital structure due to the guaranteed daily participation redemption posts a risk of bank run in the case of a negative return development. The annualized standard deviations of returns of GOEFs with more than ten years return history lie for nine out of 13 funds below one percent on average over the last ten years. Three funds realized standard deviations close to one percent, and only one fund showed more volatile returns with a standard deviation of 2.18%. Those thirteen funds make up the IPD OFIX-10[7] index which realized an annual volatility of 0.52% between 1999 and 2008 (IPD GmbH, 2009a). From an international perspective, annualised volatilities of monthly fund returns of one percent are exceptionally low. Using data of two commingled real estate funds in the US, Brueggemann et al. (1992) report annualised volatilities of 5.7% and 6.2% between 1972 and 1989. Gallo, Lockwood, and Rodriguez (2006) examine 65 pension commingled real estate funds (CREF) in the US during 1985 to 2002 of which 23 funds are open-end. Annualised standard deviations of individual fund returns ranged between 1.87% and 13.40%. The index of 23 open-end CREFs shows a standard deviation of 2.76%.

As most funds are even considered as gilt-edged investments[8], a more volatile return development like e.g. in the case of US CREFs would not be acceptable. Finally, fund management has a high *incentive to influence valuations*. Remuneration of the investment firms is based on asset volume and in many cases on the fund performance.

Given a long bear market since the German reunification in 1990 and high and stable capital influxes of most funds over the entire period, it seems possible that steadily increasing fund volumes enabled fund management to bias appraisals upwards in times of poor market conditions with a high positive influence on fund returns and readjust values back again with a lower influence on fund returns given the than higher fund volumes.

Crosby attributes smoothing and lagging tendencies in German valuations to the industry's commitment to offer a product that has very low risk and volatility and to potential influence on the valuers.

---

6 As stated in the annual report of Deka-ImmobilienFonds in 2006, p. 23.

7 Offene Fonds Immobilien Index (OFIX-10). Only those open-end funds enter the capital weighted index that have at least ten years of return history.

8 German courts considered GOEFs in various decisions as gilt-edged investments. Among the sample of 20 analysed funds, all major funds and 15 funds in total have been considered gilt-edged by at least one decision (BVI, 2009b).

Table 2.2 Factors of client influence within GOEF valuation

	Factor	Strong potential influence on appraisers	High contingency to be influenced	Influence
Characteristics of the client	Size of client	big clients > strong influence	biggest portfolios by GAV in Europe	strong
	Type of client	mortgage lenders and agents influence more than other clients	no research for GOEFs	not clear
	Sophisticated vs. unsophisticated	sophisticated clients exert information power more successful	sophisticated	strong
	Relationship with client	close relationship > strong influence	close, as few funds account for a big proportion of appraiser revenue	strong
External characteristics	Regulatory framework		no research on "margin of error" procedure in courts like in the UK	not clear
	Definition of value	well-defined definitions > weak influence	partly ambiguous (e.g. "sustainable" rents), central assumptions in WertV less transparent than in DCF approach	strong
	Market conditions of valuation industry	high competition > strong influence		not clear
Valuation characteristics	Range of defensible values	high range > strong influence	high, especially in 2006, no changes of nominal values for more than 10% of German properties	strong
	Amount of opinion	managers of complex commercial properties have high amount of opinion > strong influence	GOEFs manage complex commercial properties	strong
	Purpose of valuation	high importance of valuation result > strong influence	daily fixing of participation prices at NAV, potential of bank run, stable fund returns as central sales argument, considered as gilt-edged investment by German courts	strong
	Incentive to influence appraisal	high incentive > strong influence	remuneration performance-based, long bear market since German reunification, steady net capital influx over decades	strong

Source: Own illustration. Factors taken from Levy & Schuck (2005).

He argues that in Germany there exists no research on potential client influence on valuation[9], unlike in e.g. the US, UK or Australia and that Germany lies on a poor 12th rank on the Jones Lang LaSalle transparency index, behind a number of other European countries. Finally, Crosby concludes that: "[…] in a very long bear market, units priced by direct reference to valuations could become significantly overvalued, the situation which was perceived to exist in Germany." (Crosby 2007, p. 12).

Although research on German valuation practice is limited, it can be concluded that (1) client influence on appraisals is possible, internationally and in Germany, (2) the German valuation profession is in some regards different to the valuation profession of other countries and (3) GOEFs are an international particularity because they offer the least volatile fund returns.

2.2.2 Biased appraisals on the portfolio level

A prominent line of research addresses property valuation and its consequences on direct property performance measurement on the index level. In one of the most influential studies on direct real estate performance measurement, Geltner (1989a) presents a theory of smoothing of real estate appraisals and suggests a methodology to unsmooth property returns on the index level to reveal "real" asset volatility. He argues that two levels of smoothing can enter property index returns: Firstly, at the disaggregate level of individual property appraisals over time and secondly at the aggregate index level. He refers to the first level of smoothing as "lack of confidence" and argues that the appraiser cannot be certain if his current estimate of market value meets exactly the true market value.

He argues that given market value estimates of the same property for the previous year (as is usually the case for commingled real estate funds), appraisers will consider the previous year's estimate to at least some extent. Many subsequent studies (e.g. De Wit, 1993; Fisher, Geltner, & Webb, 1994; Geltner, 1991; Geltner, 1993; Quan & Quigley, 1991) build on Geltner's framework and refine his suggestion to "unsmooth" returns to derive the "true" direct real estate return. Corgel and deRoss (1999) show that different assumptions regarding the appraisal process and thus different models to unsmooth returns can result in very different real estate weights of an optimal multi asset portfolio. As Geltner's unsmoothing methodology relies heavily on assumptions regarding appraisal behaviour, Lai and Wang (1998) question those assumptions10 and present scenarios in which appraisal-based time series can exhibit even *more* volatility than

---

9 For example, Levy, and Schuck (2005) extend earlier research (Levy & Schuck, 1999) and find evidence for New Zealand that clients exert influence on valuers by ways of expert and information power. Wolverton and Gallimore (1999) find for US appraisers that client feedback can have an influence on appraisals.

10 Geltner, MacGregor, and Schwann (2003) concede that Lai and Wang (1998) raised a valid point in that smoothing literature had simply started from the assumption that smoothing existed. However, they do not agree upon their further argumentation.

true asset volatility, and state that: "It is unreasonable to conclude that something is wrong with appraisers just because we observe that the variance of appraisal-based returns seems artificially low." (p. 532). Their contradicting argumentation is interesting, because for German open-end funds, there exist the same return patterns (i.e. low volatility and autocorrelation) that initiated the attempts to unsmooth returns, but in the presented paper it can be shown that at least for the German properties, the assumed appraisal behaviour is not valid.

2.2.3 Return variance and portfolio diversification implications

Young (2008) updates and extends his earlier study on direct real estate return distributions of US properties (Young & Graff, 1995). The data contains annual property returns reported by the National Council of Real Estate Investment Fiduciaries (NCREIF) between 1980 and 2003. He splits up the sample by use type, anticipating that the associated variance should exceed variance stemming from regional differences. Over the entire sample, he finds the distribution to be more peaked around the mean than the corresponding normal distribution would be, having weaker shoulders and fatter tails (i.e. leptokurtic) and being negatively skewed. Interestingly, the shape of the distribution is virtually identical across property types and across regions. In the light of the infinite-variance of the return distributions, Young concludes that to obtain an acceptable degree of idiosyncratic risk reduction, funds would have to obtain nearly all investible-grade properties in the US. Graff, Harrington, and Young (1997) apply the same research design and report very similar results for property returns in Australia. Young, Lee, and Devaney (2006) use IPD UK data to conduct the same research. Findings again are very similar and the discussed consequences for portfolio optimisation severe: Given the non-normal distribution of UK property returns, a portfolio that reduces idiosyncratic risk by e.g. 90% would need to consist out of 1,698 properties. In contrast, in case of normally distributed returns, the same risk reduction could be achieved with only 100 properties.

The main caveat of the mentioned studies regarding return distribution is the omission of the portfolio ownership of the properties as explanatory variable or at least as a possibility to split up the sample. This disadvantage in research design can be regarded as the price the authors have to pay for relying on easily accessible, good quality data that is yet confidential. A recent study of Kurzrock, Gläsner, and Wilke (2009) addresses the fund performance of all 118 German open-end retail and special funds. They use publicly available information and find that funds targeting institutional investors tend to outperform funds targeting retail investors. Their findings indicate that portfolio ownership is a central variable for real estate performance in Germany. However, they do not address individual property performance, as it is the case within the presented paper.

2.3 *Data and research method*

2.3.1 Data

The main innovation of the presented dataset is its non-confidentiality. In contrast to the above cited studies with datasets collected by the European Association for Investors in Non-listed Real Estate Funds (INREV) or IPD, the presented data is publicly available from the accounts of the German open-end real estate retail funds. As a consequence, the research design can aim for a maximum of explanatory power without consideration of interests from particular parties such as the funds as portfolio holders.

For the purpose of this paper the annual reports of 24 GOEFs funds have been analyzed for the years 2004 to 2007. For 2004, only seven funds published the required data, for 2005 already 15 and for 2006 and 2007 all 24 funds. As reporting months differ among the funds, the analysis needs to shift report data from the first half of the year into the previous years' analysis period[11]. In total, 69 annual reports have been analyzed. Funds publish information on various aspects of their property investments on the individual property level, but the level of detail varies by fund. For all funds, crucial characteristics within the appraisal process could be retrieved: Occupancy rate, date of purchase[12] and the percentage of leases that end within the next twelve months.

To investigate the variance of appraisals between two years on a relative basis, the change in the market value of one property between two years is calculated. This procedure requires two market values of the same property in two subsequent years to obtain the change in market value (DMV). For those properties which were part of the portfolios for two or more subsequent years and that were not under development within that time, the change in market value is calculated:

$$DMV_{t1} = \frac{MV_{t1}}{MV_{t0}} - 1 \tag{2.1}$$

Where DMV_{t1} denotes the percentage change in market values and MV_{t1} and MV_{t0} are the market values reported in two subsequent annual statements of accounts. As we are interested in the property appraisals rather than on aggregated property performance on portfolio level, we do not weight value changes by capital.

---

11 This means that report information from e.g. January 31, 2007 would be included into the analysis year 2006, as eleven out of twelve months of fund or property performance fall into 2006.

12 Alternatively to the date of purchase, the building year (historical or economic) could be used as well. As funds consider themselves as core investments, they usually buy fully let and newly built properties. Therefore, the variables are closely related in most cases with the exception of developments that result in a newer economic construction year. A more detailed explanation for the inclusion of the independent variables will be presented in the following section.

This means that each property has the same influence on mean value changes within our dataset, regardless of its market value.

Capital investments would increase the market value and have to be accounted for. Unfortunately, funds do not publish information on capital investments on the individual property level[13], but they consistently report the state of investment. With the exclusion of properties under development, the remaining standing investments are those with no or at least only limited capital investments, such that the approximation of the change in market value between two years can be interpret as the value change of the property driven by external factors. In the given research context with strong value gains of German properties as reported by market agents (Figure 2.1) and strong property devaluations within some of the GOEFs, the negligence of minor capital investments is even less important, as those investments would have increased the property values. The observed devaluations would have been even more extreme if capital investments had occurred.

After the exclusion of non-German properties and properties under development, 1,334 changes in value of German properties remain (Table 2.3). All value changes are weighted equally, which means that the market value of a property does not matter when comparing e.g. mean value changes by portfolio. In the three analysis years, between 338 (2005) and 512 (2007) value changes are calculated. The corresponding properties account for an aggregated value of 12.1 bn. EUR in 2005 to 20.2 bn. EUR in 2007.

2.3.2 Research method

2.3.2.1 Differentiating value changes by portfolio ownership

German open-end real estate retail funds are strictly regulated by the Investment Act (2008). In the context of the paper, the most relevant regulations exist with respect to diversification and (maximum) leverage requirements. The funds themselves claim to offer a diversified real estate investment with a low risk profile and stable returns. Funds differ with respect to global asset allocation, but regarding their investment style *within* Germany hardly any differences exist.

The sample includes office and retail properties that are primarily located within the major German property markets. Due to sample size restrictions, the properties have not been split up by property type or region.

---

13 Thomas (1997) derives a performance index for the German property market also using the statements of accounts of GOEFs. At this time, funds reported only aggregated property values and on the aggregate level, capital investments can be incorporated to better estimate standing investment performance.

Table 2.3 Number and market values of properties between 2005 and 2007

	2005		2006		2007	
Fund	**Sum MV (in EUR)**	**# MV**	**Sum MV (in EUR)**	**# MV**	**Sum MV (in EUR)**	**# MV**
AXA IMMOSELECT			242,312,000	9	388,679,000	10
CS EUROREAL					1,659,120,000	39
DEGI EUROPA					1,248,560,000	16
Deka-Immo.Europa	1,609,620,000	27	1,584,349,000	28	1,348,370,000	27
Deka-Immo.Global	129,790,000	2				
Deka-Immo.Fonds	4,095,137,091	129	3,457,142,739	126	3,159,100,000	115
EURO ImmoProfil					1,595,280,000	71
grundbesitz-europa	4,017,193,000	98	2,468,795,000	66	316,089,000	3
HANSAimmobilia					171,385,000	19
HAUSINV. europa			1,485,208,000	26	1,522,335,000	25
INTER ImmoProfil					338,680,000	13
M.S. P2 VALUE					68,480,000	2
SEB ImmoInvest			1,855,100,000	62	1,458,300,000	38
TMW Immo. Wf.					90,880,000	2
UBS (D) Euroinvest			623,700,000	22	437,500,000	15
UniImmo: D.			3,647,410,000	57	1,967,550,000	22
UniImmo: Europa					1,715,310,000	25
UniImmo: Global			242,881,000	2	363,015,000	3
WestInvest 1	1,812,495,100	71	1,815,168,000	72	1,552,138,000	52
WestInvest InterS.	442,226,000	11	612,369,000	14	816,655,000	15
Total	**12,106,461,191**	**338**	**18,034,434,739**	**484**	**20,217,426,000**	**512**
Min.	129,790,000	2	242,312,000	2	68,480,000	2
Max.	4,095,137,091	129	3,647,410,000	126	3,159,100,000	115

Since the correlation coefficients of capital growth rates between the IPD office sector and the "all properties" sector (0.966) and between the retail sector and the "all properties" sector (0.726) are very high[14], the omission of this factor seems admissible. For the sectors industrial and residential however, correlation coefficients are much lower (0.072 and 0.418), but GOEFs are not invested in this property type (IPD GmbH, 2009a). The correlation coefficients of the capital growth rates of the IPD "all properies" segment and the regional office segments[15] Berlin, Düsseldorf, Frankfurt, Hamburg, Cologne, Munich and Stuttgart range between 0.57 in case of Hamburg and 0.94 for Munich. Therefore, the omission of the variable location within Germany seems to be acceptable as well.

The expectation is that the value changes of the German properties do not differ significantly by portfolio. The following research hypothesis is tested:

H0: "All means of value changes of German properties over all portfolios are equal"

Although for individual properties value changes in contrast to the general market development are possible, it is assumed that in line with the idea of portfolio diversification those individual deviations should level out in the portfolio context. A rejection of the null hypothesis would imply that either there existed an influence from funds on the valuation of their properties or that the portfolios differed substantially with respect to factors that influenced value changes in 2006. In the first case, valuation would not take place independently as required by the Investment Act (2008). In the second case, the consequence would be that the degree of diversification of the funds' German properties is not sufficient in the sense that it resembles developments of the German property market. In terms of risk diversification, there would remain a significant degree of unsystematic property risk within the thought-to-be fully diversified portfolios. An unvaried analysis of variance (ANOVA) tests the potential influence of funds on property valuation.

2.3.2.2 Attributing value changes to portfolio characteristics

To test whether portfolio characteristics had an influence on property value changes (DMV) in 2006, a linear regression model is derived:

$$DMV_{t1} \sim \alpha_1 + \alpha_2 OCR_{t1} + \alpha_3 year.of.purchase + \alpha_4 perc.ending.leases_{t1} + \varepsilon \qquad (2.2)$$

---

14 IPD Germany has data for the years 1991 to 2008 (IPD GmbH, 2009b).

15 The regional data is available only from 1996 onward and only for the office and residential segment, not for the all property segment.

Where α_1 denotes the constant and ε the error term. The three factors vacancy rate (as OCR for occupancy rate), holding period (as year.of.purchase) and lease structure (as perc.ending.leases) are labelled α_2 to α_4. Those three factors are directly derived for all funds from the statements of accounts.

In the presence of deteriorating lease market conditions[16], a high vacancy rate and a high percentage of ending lease contracts should result in an increased valuation discount (and vice versa for improving market conditions). The factor *change in vacancy rate* is not included in the accounts, but could easily be calculated. However, it will not enter the model. Firstly, because of data limitations, as to calculate a change in vacancy rates, the vacancy rates of two years are needed. Unfortunately, for many portfolios, information on vacancy rates has been included only in recent years, such that the sample size would diminish strongly (see section 2.4.3 for a detailed discussion).

A second argument for not including the change in vacancy rate is that this factor would be the only factor for which an effect on market values is assumed within the normative valuation process. If the vacancy rate increases, in many cases this will mean an information update from t_0 to t_1 and thus, all other things equal, a discount on the market value would be expected. For all other point in time factors however, in the presence of a free valuation process of correctly valued properties in t_0, there should be no effects on valuation in t_1. For example the mere existence of a high vacancy rate in 2006 should not result in a significant valuation discount in 2006, because the discount should have entered the valuation already in the year when the vacancy occurred.

2.4 Results

2.4.1 Value changes by portfolio ownership

The means of property value changes over all portfolios as a group differ considerably between the years 2005 to 2007 (Table 2.4). In 2005 the average property lost 4.3% in value, with a standard deviation of 6.2% over the 338 analyzed properties. In 2006, the observed market downturn accelerated to -8.4% and the standard deviation among the 484 properties reached 13.1%, more than twice the value of 2005. In 2007, value changes are still negative, but with an average of only -1.7%. The standard deviation among the 512 properties falls back to 5.8%, which is about the range that was present in 2005. Especially the fact that the strongest devaluations occurred in 2006 is in contrast to the transaction market evidence (Figure 2.1) which reports the strongest yield compression for 2006.

16 Deteriorating expectations about future lease market conditions should as well result in a valuation discount, but this variable can not be observed.

The distribution of DMV is not normal. The normality tests[17] of Jarque-Bera, Anderson-Darling and Shapiro-Wilk reject normality at the 0.01 significance level for all years.

Table 2.4 Distribution of changes in market values between 2005 and 2007

DMV	Analysis year		
	2005	2006	2007
# Properties	338	484	512
Mean (in %)	-4.287	-8.411	-1.716
Standard deviation (in %)	6.156	13.129	5.752
Skewness	-1.595	-2.038	-1.396
Kurtosis	6.806	5.764	7.697

Table 2.5 shows statistics for property valuations from 2005 to 2007 by funds. The portfolio sizes of the German properties differ substantially in all three years between two (min.) and 129 (max.) properties. In most of the cases, the distribution is not normal. In 2005, for all six portfolios with exception of grundbesitz-europa all three tests reject normality at the 0.05 level. In 2006, normality is rejected by all three tests for six out of ten funds.

For all portfolios with more than ten observations, again with the exception of grundbesitz-europa, normality is rejected by at least one of the three tests. Grundbesitz-europa seems to be a special case in 2005 and 2006, as the distribution is neither very skewed nor has excess kurtosis. In 2007 at least one test rejects normality at the 0.1 level for 13 out of 14 funds with more than ten German properties.

The possibility to split up the sample by portfolio has proven to be valuable. Especially in 2006, the disparity of value changes between portfolios is extremely high. Despite the heterogeneity of property value changes among portfolios, even the growth rates of the portfolio with the highest mean value changes, AXA IMMOSELECT with plus 2.3%, are still much lower than the reported yield compression would suggest (Table 2.5). The value changes of the entire group of 20 GOEFs are in contrast to market developments inferred from the transaction market.The cross-sectional standard deviation of the entire sample of 484 properties value changes is 13.1% in 2006 (Table 2.4).

Table 2.5 shows that the high value results primarily from one single portfolio, namely Deka-ImmobilienFonds, with a standard deviation of 18.5% and a mean of -18.0%.

17 The three chosen standard normality tests differ in terms of how they test distributions for normality. Some tests rely on the measures of skewness and kurtosis while others compare the distribution in terms of functional aspects. For a detailed review of strengths and weaknesses of normality tests, please refer to D'Agostino, Belanger, and D'Agostino Jr. (1990).

Table 2.5 Changes in market values between 2005 and 2007 by funds

	2005					2006					2007				
Fund	#	Mean	Sd.	Skew.	Kurt.	#	Mean	Sd.	Skew.	Kurt.	#	Mean	Sd.	Skew.	Kurt.
AXA IMMOS.						9	0.023	0.03	0.479	-1.441	10	0.009	0.03	0.259	-1.188
CS EUROREAL											39	-0.012	0.05	1.707	9.102
DEGI EUROPA											16	-0.021	0.10	-0.511	1.383
Deka-Immo.Europa	27	-0.033	0.04	-1.998	3.499	28	-0.095	0.10	-1.098	1.160	27	-0.026	0.05	-1.937	5.783
Deka-Immo.Global	2	-0.075	0.10	0.000	-2.750	0					0				
Deka-Immo.Fonds	129	-0.050	0.06	-1.576	6.621	126	-0.180	0.18	-0.833	0.946	115	-0.017	0.05	-2.621	12.66
EURO ImmoProfil											71	-0.019	0.04	-0.632	2.873
grundbesitz-europa	98	-0.040	0.05	-0.180	0.630	66	-0.111	0.07	0.101	-0.365	3	0.002	0.00	-0.017	-2.333
HANSAimmobilia											19	-0.027	0.05	-0.436	1.611
HAUSINV. europa						26	-0.080	0.14	-2.445	5.517	25	-0.014	0.06	-0.101	2.141
INTER ImmoProfil											13	0.004	0.01	1.044	0.297
M.S. P2 VALUE											2	0.009	0.00	0.000	-2.750
SEB ImmoInvest						62	-0.030	0.05	-2.861	10.31	38	-0.013	0.03	-1.642	3.973
TMW Immo. Wf.											2	0.029	0.01	0.000	-2.750
UBS (D) Euroinv.						22	0.002	0.05	0.236	0.149	15	-0.001	0.04	0.948	0.416
UniImmo: D.						57	-0.035	0.08	-3.475	14.90	22	-0.027	0.08	-0.931	3.342
UniImmo: Europa											25	-0.020	0.07	-1.435	2.066
UniImmo: Global						2	0.003	0.00	0.000	-2.750	3	0.016	0.02	0.385	-2.333
WestInvest 1	71	-0.039	0.06	-2.621	10.45	72	-0.028	0.04	-1.627	2.797	52	-0.033	0.06	-1.446	2.266
WestInvest InterS.	11	-0.025	0.05	-2.020	3.127	14	-0.021	0.04	-0.296	-0.404	15	-0.008	0.03	-0.812	0.184
All properties	338	-0.042	0.06	-1.595	6.806	484	-0.084	0.13	-2.038	5.764	512	-0.017	0.05	-1.396	7.697

For the two Deka funds and the fund HAUS-INVEST europa, intra-portfolio variance is twice as high in 2006 as in 2007. For three funds however, variance in 2006 is lower or equal to 2007 and for the remaining three funds with sufficient data variance is higher in 2006 but to a minor extent. Nine out of eleven portfolios have a standard deviation below the 13.1% of the entire sample, and six portfolios have standard deviations of about five percent or less. While Young and Graff (1995) found with respect to US CREFs that the distribution of property value changes does not differ across geographic regions and property types (see section 2.2.3), for GOEFs it is evident that the distributions vary vastly by portfolio. For this variable however, the mentioned studies could not account for due to data confidentiality.

Besides the already mentioned differences with respect to the mean and the standard deviation, the distributions differ extremely with regard to higher moments as well. While the skewness parameter of the distribution of all properties is negative in all three years with values between -1.4 and -2.0, some portfolios like CS EUROREAL or UBS (D) Euroinvest show positive parameter values. The same is true for the kurtosis of the distributions. Portfolios like AXA IMMOSELECT or grundbesitz-europa have a platykurtic distribution of changes in market values, while the distribution of all properties is characterised by a leptokurtic kurtosis parameter of 5.7.

When Graff, Harrington, and Young (1997) conclude for the UK market that given the high variance of individual property returns almost all property portfolios have to be considered poorly diversified, the presented evidence on the German market gives reason to reconsider their findings. At least for the properties of German open-end retail fund portfolios, portfolio ownership[18] is an important variable for value change variance and distribution and should not be neglected for the estimation of idiosyncratic property risk.

The rejection of normality and the differences in the distributions of property value changes by funds require cautious interpretation of the significance levels of ANOVA results. However, we find for 2006 significant differences of DMV in excess of the 99.9% level (Table 2.6), and non-parametric Wilcoxon Signed Rank Test results confirm t-test results (Figure 2.2).

Therefore, the **null hypothesis of equal value changes by portfolios can be rejected for 2006**. Adjusted R Squared reaches 23.5%, which can be considered as a high explanatory power, given the cross-sectional character of the univariate analysis over just one period.

18 When analysing the influence of property characteristics on office property performance using the IPD Germany database, Kurzrock, Rottke, and Schiereck (2009) find the variable portfolio ownership highly significant as well.

Table 2.6 ANOVA of changes in market values in 2006

Tests of Between-Subjects Effects for 2006
Dependent Variable: DMV

Source	Type III Sum of Squares	Df	Mean Square	F	Sig.	Partial Eta Squared
Corrected Model	20909.3	10	2090.9	15.862	.000	.251
Intercept	3505.3	1	3505.1	26.592	.000	.053
fund name	20909.3	10	2090.9	15.862	.000	.251
Error	62350.6	473	131.819			
Total	117500.6	484				
Corrected Total	83259.9	483				

R Squared = .251 (Adjusted R Squared = .235)

Although the observed means of DMV differ substantially among funds in all three years, **the research hypothesis cannot be rejected for the year 2005 and 2007.** In both years, the model clearly misses statistical significances with p-values of 0.677 (2007) and 0.483 (2005). A closer look at the 95% confidence intervals reveals that limited sample size, low mean differences and high variance of value changes within funds impede differences in means from gaining significance in 2007 (Figure 2.3). In 2006, differences between marginal means range from -18.0% to 2.3%, with standard deviations within fund portfolios below 3.9% in nine out of ten cases (Figure 2.2).

Results differ largely and as expected between funds in fund crisis year 2006 versus 2005 and 2007. For 2005, the means of value changes differ statistically significant between portfolios. If German direct property performance is to be analyzed in 2006, portfolio ownership should not be omitted as analysis has shown that the sample is too heterogeneous and biased in the sense that few portfolios experienced extremely negative value changes over the majority of their properties. With respect to the eleven portfolios available for analysis in 2006, we find that the Deka-ImmobilienFonds portfolio[19] is isolated as the mean value change of properties lies with 5% error likelihood below the second worse performing portfolio grundbesitz-europa. Deka-ImmobilienEuropa, grundbesitz-europa and HAUS-INVEST europa form a second group of value changes within a similar range. The remaining seven portfolios still differ substantially in mean value changes, but in most cases differences between portfolios do not reach the 0.05 significance level.

19 Deka Bank guaranteed investors of Deka-ImmobilienFonds a minimum return of 2% for 2006, a unique procedure among German open-end funds. Without that guarantee being granted, property depreciations in excess of 700 mill. EUR would have resulted in a fund return of about -7%, as Deka Bank reports a subsidy effect of 9.1% with respect to the fund return (Annual report 2006, p. 24).

Figure 2.2 Confidence intervals of property value changes in 2006

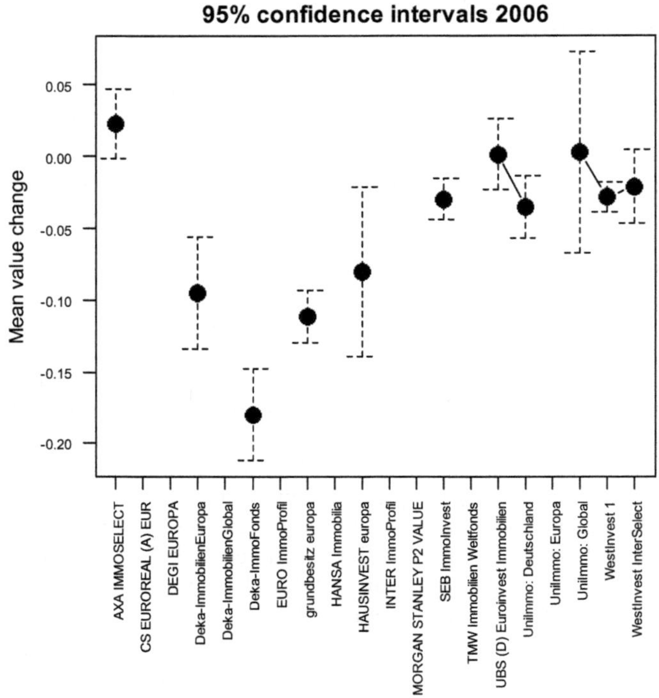

2.4.2 Attribution of value changes by portfolio characteristics

The regression model to explain property value changes by portfolio characteristics (section 2.3.2.2) includes the year of purchase, the occupancy rate and the percentage of ending leases as independent variables.

Unfortunately, not all variables are available for every single property; especially information on the percentage of ending leases is omitted for many properties. Therefore, within the complete three-variable model, some properties have been excluded from analysis.

Table 2.7 summarizes the variables that are relevant for the design of the regression model. With respect to the regression requirement of equal group variances, the changes of the standard deviations of variables from one year to the other are interesting. It is striking that only those variables show a strongly increased standard deviation in 2006 that are determined in the valuation process. The standard deviation of the yield change DYP increases from 4.4% in 2005 to 9.7% in 2006 and falls back to 4.0% in 2007.

Figure 2.3 Confidence intervals of property value changes in 2007

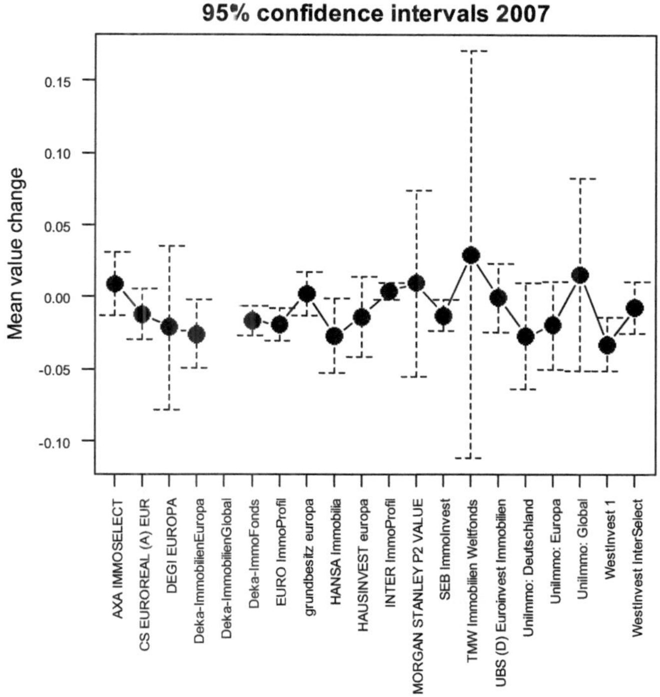

For the change of the rental value, standard deviation increases from 4.9% in 2005 to 8.4% in 2006 and falls back to 4.6% in 2007. The strongest change shows the change in market value. Its standard deviation increases from 6.2% in 2005 to 13.1% in 2006 and goes down to 5.8% in 2007. Those variables that are not affected by the valuation process in contrast, namely the occupancy rate, the change in occupancy rate and the percentage of ending leases, do not change noticeably within the three years.

Since the variance of some variables has changed dramatically in the year 2006, Levene's test has been conducted to see whether variable variance differs significantly by fund. For the year 2006, the test is rejected at the 0.01 significance level for all variables except DOCR and perc.ending.leases. In 2007, equal group variance is only rejected for year.of.purchase, occupancy.rate and YP. An interesting fact is again that the test does not reject equal variance for the variables change in occupancy rate and the percentage of ending leases, which are not determined by the valuation process.

Table 2.7 Regression model to explain changes in market values

2005	Mean	Sd.	N	NA
year.of.purchase	1993.2	8.6	338	0
occupancy.rate	0.821	0.243	251	87
DOCR	-0.019	0.145	97	241
perc.ending.leases	0.142	0.248	251	87
YP	14.98	2.45	337	1
DYP	-0.010	0.044	336	2
DERV	-0.034	0.049	336	2
DMV	-0.043	0.062	338	0
2006				
year.of.purchase	1993.9	9.0	484	0
occupancy.rate	0.831	0.241	474	10
DOCR	-0.009	0.152	378	106
perc.ending.leases	0.128	0.219	379	105
YP	14.50	2.86	471	13
DYP	-0.039	0.097	471	13
DERV	-0.051	0.084	471	13
DMV	-0.084	0.131	484	0
2007				
year.of.purchase	1995.1	8.7	512	0
occupancy.rate	0.843	0.243	442	70
DOCR	-0.011	0.139	428	84
perc.ending.leases	0.141	0.198	284	228
YP	14.94	2.74	496	16
DYP	-0.004	0.040	494	18
DERV	-0.013	0.046	494	18
DMV	-0.017	0.058	512	0

The table reports input variables of the linear regression DMV ~ occupancy.rate + year.of.purchase + perc.ending.leases.

The analysis of variable variance has shown that especially in 2006 those variables that are affected by the appraisal process strongly increase in variance and differ in terms of group variance by funds. The fact that the variance of important valuation input factors like the occupancy rate, the change in occupancy rate and the percentage of ending leases does not increase in 2006 and does not differ by funds strengthens the assumption that the appraisal process in 2006 was different within some funds, or in other words, that at least some funds influenced valuation at least in 2006. Table 2.8 summarizes the results of the linear regression model[20] subdivided by fund. The bold figures indicate significance at the 0.1 level, while italics indicate that the sign of the empirical estimate deviates from model expectations.

20 The variance inflation factor is below 2 for all models, therefore multicollinarity is of no relevant concern. Nevertheless, given the controversy of results, we account explicitly for heteroscedasticity. All standard errors are adjusted using White's (1980) covariance matrix for all regression models.

Table 2.8 Changes in market values in 2006 by portfolio characteristics

Fund	Model			Variables		
	p-value	Df	Adj. R squared	occupancy. rate	year.of. purchase	perc.ending. leases
Deka Immo.Europa	**0.052**	24	0.427	**0.207**	0.017	*0.098*
				(2.050)	(1.543)	(0.245)
Deka-Immo.Fonds	**0.000**	113	0.374	**0.361**	0.001	**-0.148**
				(4.949)	(0.751)	**(-2.160)**
grundbesitz-europa	**0.008**	62	0.243	**0.168**	*-0.001*	-0.005
				(2.942)	(-0.937)	(-0.067)
HAUSINV. europa	0.397	11	0.467	0.172	0.004	-0.367
				(0.700)	(0.571)	(-0.660)
SEB ImmoInvest	0.152	17	0.351	0.097	*-0.001*	-0.073
				(1.457)	(-0.653)	(-0.614)
UBS (D) Euroinv.	**0.094**	17	0.149	**0.110**	***-0.016***	-0.003
				(2.305)	**(-2.272)**	(-0.052)
UniImmo: D.	0.149	53	0.218	0.035	0.001	-0.151
				(0.465)	(1.472)	(-1.273)
WestInvest 1	**0.012**	35	0.059	0.011	0.001	-0.048
				(0.131)	(0.466)	(-1.602)
WestInvest InterS.	0.532	5	-0.191	0.023	*-0.010*	-0.063
				(0.108)	(-0.513)	(-1.411)

The table reports results of the linear regression DMV ~ occupancy.rate + year.of.purchase + perc.ending.leases. The three columns to the left report p-values, degrees of freedom and adjusted R squared values of the model, while the three columns to the right state the estimates of the independent variables. Figures in parentheses under the corresponding estimates report the t-values. Bold coefficients imply a p-value of 0.1 or lower.

For five out of nine funds, the model is significant at the 0.1 level. Deka-ImmobilienFonds and grundbesitz-europa have 116 and 65 complete datasets (i.e. all three variables could be retrieved) for 2006 and the model is significant at the 0.01 level. SEB ImmoInvest and UBS (D) Euroinvest Immobilien have only 20 complete observations and closely miss the 0.1 significance level. However, although UniImmo: Deutschland has third most observations (56) among all funds in 2006, the model does not reach significance.The model explains from 5.9% of sample variance in the case of WestInvest 1 (adjusted R squared) to as much as 42.7% in the case of Deka-ImmobilienEuropa. The facts that almost all estimates have the anticipated signs and the partly high R squared values indicate that for many funds the models fit the data well. However, in most cases the t-values of the variables year.of.purchase and perc.ending.leases are not significant, in many cases far off from this. In a second step the model is reformulated in order to include only those variables that are significant for each fund (Table 2.9).

Table 2.9 Changes in market values in 2006 explained by best fit model

	Model			Variables		
Fund	p-value	Df	Adj. R squared	occupancy. rate	year.of. purchase	perc.ending. leases
AXA IMMOS.	**0.001**	7	0.891		**-0.024** (-5.304)	
Deka Immo.Europa	**0.011**	25	0.436	**0.181** (2.668)	0.018 (1.671)	
Deka-Immo.Fonds	**0.000**	113	0.374	**0.361** (4.949)	0.001 (0.751)	**-0.148** (-2.160)
grundbesitz-europa	**0.000**	64	0.255	**0.166** (3.941)		
HAUSINV. europa	**0.072**	24	0.388	**0.413** (1.880)		
SEB ImmoInvest	**0.002**	60	0.106	**0.081** (3.159)		
UBS (D) Euroinv.	**0.044**	18	0.197	**0.111** (2.274)	**-0.016** (-2.295)	
UniImmo: D.	0.145	55	0.227			-0.164 (-1.478)
WestInvest 1	**0.002**	69	0.196	0.061 (1.457)	**0.003** (1.995)	
WestInvest InterS.	0.953	11	-0.159	0.026 (0.215)	-0.005 (-0.287)	

The table reports results of the linear regression DMV ~ occupancy.rate + year.of.purchase + perc.ending.leases for those funds for which all three variables are significant. Insignificant variables have been excluded from the model. Figures in parentheses under the corresponding estimates report the t-values. Bold coefficients imply a p-value of 0.1 or lower.

For all funds except Deka-ImmobilienFonds one or two non significant variables are excluded. The omission of the variable perc.ending.leases increases for many funds the number of complete observations and also the degrees of freedom. In case of AXA IMMOSELECT, the omission of the variable perc.ending.leases leads to 9 complete datasets, while in the case of the complete three-variable model this fund could not be included. The total number of observations of all now ten funds increases to 461 from only 364 in the complete model.

In the adapted model, eight out of ten models reach the 0.1 significance level, three even reach 0.01 significance. The adjusted R squared values range between 10.1% (SEB ImmoInvest) and 43.6% (Deka-ImmobilienFonds) and all estimates except two have the anticipated signs. In case of AXA IMMOSELECT, the only significant variable is year.of.purchase, but the estimator sign is opposed to the model expectation. UniImmo: Deutschland is an exception as the model again closely misses the 0.1 significance level despite a high number (56) of observations. Different from all other funds, the most significant variable is not the occupancy.rate, but the percentage of ending leases. For three funds, only the variable occupancy.rate is significant, but still can explain 25.5%

(grundbesitz-europa), 38.9% (HAUS-INVEST europa) and 10.6% (SEB ImmoInvest) of variance in property value changes in 2006.

In 2005 only Deka-ImmobilienEuropa, Deka-ImmobilienFonds and grundbesitz-europa included information on occupancy rates in their statements of accounts. All three funds show a similar pattern with respect to explained sample variance, estimate signs and magnitude of significant estimates. The model for Deka-ImmobilienEuropa with only 26 properties closely misses the 0.1 significance level, while the models for the two other funds are significant at the 0.01 significance level. The variable occupancy rate is significant for all funds, while the percentage of ending leases is only significant for grundbesitz-europa. In comparison to 2006, the model explains less variance in the case of Deka-ImmobilienEuropa (32.8% vs. 42.7%) and Deka-ImmobilienFonds (32.5% vs. 37.4%), but slightly more in case of grundbesitz-europa (28.1% vs. 24.3%). The estimates for the variable occupancy rate are lower in 2005 for all three funds: Deka-ImmobilienEuropa 0.083 vs. 0.207, Deka-ImmobilienFonds 0.133 vs. 0.361 and grundbesitz-europa 0.126 vs. 0.168.

In 2007 all funds publish data on individual property level, but either omission of information on the percentage of ending leases or total disinvestment in Germany led to the exclusion of many funds. The sample grows from ten funds in 2006 to 13 funds in 2007, but caused by disinvestment and reduced data publication of indirect property holdings, the number of properties in the sample decreases from 486 in 2006 to 223 in 2007. This leaves only four funds with more than 20 observations, and only for those four funds the model becomes statistically significant. Although the full model reaches significance in 2007 only for four funds, it can be concluded that the relation between occupancy rates and value changes in 2007 was much weaker than in 2006 and differed substantially by fund.

2.4.3 Accounting for the change in the occupancy rate

Analysis has shown that the occupancy rate is by far the most relevant variable to explain value changes especially in 2006. Although it has been argued in the beginning that the change in occupancy rate (DOCR) is not included into the regression model as an additional variable, the following section addresses the possibility that the decrease in occupancy rate rather than the level of occupancy itself might be the true cause for value declines of (partly) vacant properties.

Table 2.10 contrasts the variables occupancy rate versus change in occupancy rate. In the years 2004 and 2005 not all funds reported vacancy rates on individual property level. Therefore, in 2005 the variable DOCR is only available for 97 properties, in contrast to 251 properties where OCR is available. The ratio of DOCR / OCR improves from 38.6% in 2005 to 79.7% in 2006 and in 2007 variable availability is almost equal (96.8%). Interestingly, in about one third of the cases where DOCR is available, the variable is zero, which means that no changes in vacancy rates from one year to the next occurred. For most properties, this was the case when the building was fully let (100%) in both points of time. In 42.3% (2006) of the cases, DOCR is positive, meaning that the occupancy increased. From a perspective that considers only the direction (and not the extent) of changes in occupancy rate, it can be stated that 2006 was a good year in terms of reduction of vacancies, because for 73.5% of properties the level of vacancy either decreased or remained unchanged.

Fehler! Ungültiger Eigenverweis auf Textmarke. confirms those findings. The mean of OCR improves[21] from 82.1% in 2005 to 83.1% in 2006 to 84.3% in 2007, and also the median constantly improves. However, the fact that in all three years more than one quarter of all properties have vacancy rates in excess of 20% shows that vacancy is a relevant issue for many buildings.

The comparison of both variables has shown two important characteristics with respect to the inclusion into the regression model:

- Inclusion of the variable DOCR would have resulted in a reduction of the sample size from 474 to 378 observations in 2006
- In 73.5% of the cases, DOCR is zero or positive. This means that for those cases an effect of the level of occupancy (OCR) rate on the change of market value (DMV) cannot be explained by an simultaneous increase in vacancy rate (DOCR)
- Figure 2.4 illustrates that as well in the sample with a positive or no change in the occupancy rate (sample A, DOCR>=0, left graph) as in the sample with a negative change in occupancy rate (sample B, DOCR<0, right graph) there exists a positive relation between the *level of occupancy rate* and the change in market value. However, the relation is more intense for the sample with the negative *change in OCR*. The correlation coefficient of OCR and DMV is 0.412 for sample A and 0.627 for sample B.

Table 2.12 shows regression results of the linear model already introduced in section 2.4.2, split up between the two sub samples. If sample size was not of central concern in the given context, the sub sample of those cases where the change in occupancy rate was zero or positive would be preferable to the entire sample of all levels of occupancy rate, regardless of the change (Table 2.8), because for sub sample A (Table 2.12, upper part) with DOCR>=0 the effect of the level of vacancy is isolated from potential (and inseparable) influence from the change in vacancy. Unfortunately, with the decrease in sample size the regression model is only significant at the 0.05 level for Deka-ImmobilienEuropa and Deka-ImmobilienFonds.

21 The inclusion of several new funds in 2006 and 2007 implies a potential sample bias such that intertemporal comparisons have only limited reliability.

Table 2.10 Change in occupancy rate vs. occupancy rate

	# Properties	# Occupancy rate available	# Change in occupancy rate available	% Change in occupancy rate available	# Constant occupancy rate	# Increased occupancy rate	# Decreased occupancy rate	% Constant occupancy rate	% Increased occupancy rate	% Decreased occupancy rate
2005	338	251	97	38.6%	24	33	40	24.7%	34.0%	41.2%
2006	484	474	378	79.7%	118	160	100	31.2%	42.3%	26.5%
2007	512	442	428	96.8%	140	158	130	32.7%	36.9%	30.4%
2005-2007	1,334	1,167	903	77.4%	282	351	270	31.2%	38.9%	29.9%

Table 2.11 Occupancy rates between 2005 and 2007

	# Properties	NA	Min.	1st 25%	Median	Mean	3rd 25%	Max.
2005	338	87	0.000	0.767	0.915	0.821	1.000	1.000
2006	484	10	0.000	0.741	0.950	0.831	1.000	1.000
2007	512	70	0.000	0.789	0.970	0.843	1.000	1.000
2005-2007	1,334	167	0.000	0.767	0.952	0.833	1.000	1.000

Figure 2.4 Occupancy rate vs. capital growth 2006, by change in occupancy rate

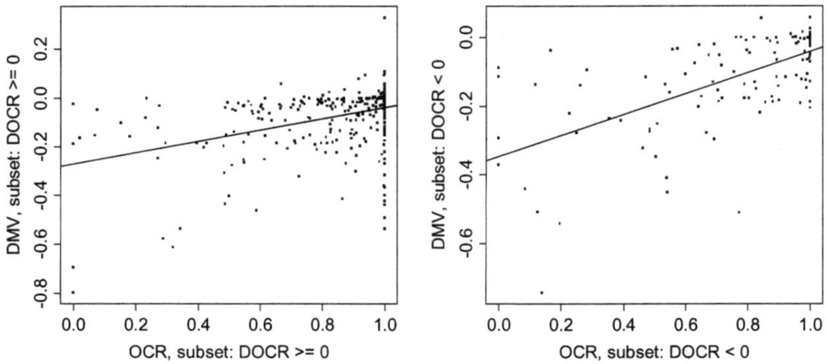

For the remaining six funds for which an estimate for the variable occupancy rate could be calculated, the sign of the estimate is at least positive as expected. The fact that the model becomes significant for Deka-ImmobilienEuropa with only 18 properties but completely misses significance for UniImmo: Deutschland with 39 properties again shows that the value changes of properties also depend on the portfolio ownership. In case of both Deka funds, the level of vacancy rates seems to have had an important influence on valuation in 2006, while for UniImmo: Deutschland this influence cannot be observed. For Deka-ImmobilienFonds, the extent of the influence surprises: An estimate of 0.297 can be interpret as for one percentage point of vacancy rate, properties were devaluated by 0.297 percentage points.

For sub sample B with DOCR<0 (Table 2.12, lower part) the model also becomes significant for two funds, namely Deka-ImmobilienFonds again and grundbesitz-europa. The estimates for the variable occupancy rate are much higher than in sample A and again all estimate signs are positive as expected. However, in sub sample B the effect on market value cannot be separated between the *level of occupancy rate* and the *change of occupancy rate*.

2.5 *Conclusion*

The first analysis of the distribution of appraisals of properties held by GOEFs has shown significant differences of property valuation between funds' portfolios in fund crisis year 2006. Nevertheless, the value changes of the entire group of 20 GOEFs are in contrast to market developments inferred from the transaction market. Funds claim to have diversified their assets to eliminate unsystematic risk and follow similar investment strategies with respect to their asset allocation within Germany.

Table 2.12 Model comparison: DOCR>=0 vs. DOCR<0

Year = 2006	Model			occupancy.rate				year.of.purchase				perc.ending.leases			
Fund	p-value	Df	Adjusted R squared	Exp. Sign Estimate	Estimate	Std. Error	t value	Exp. Sign Estimate	Estimate	Std. Error	t value	Exp. Sign Estimate	Estimate	Std. Error	Pr(>|t|)
Model: DMV ~ occupancy.rate+year.of.purchase+perc.ending.leases with DOCR >= 0															
AXA IMMOS.		NA		+				+				-			
Deka-Immo.E.	0.035**	18	0.287	+	0.151	0.132	1.151	+	0.010	0.010	1.053	-	0.050	0.167	0.769
Deka-Immo.Fonds	0.000***	80	0.254	+	0.297	0.125	2.368**	+	0.001	0.002	0.791	-	-0.191	0.074	0.012
grundbesitz-europa	0.139	32	0.158	+	0.114	0.051	2.219**	+	-0.001	0.001	-0.394	-	-0.054	0.176	0.763
HAUSINV. europa	0.473	8	0.545	+	0.216	0.302	0.716	+	0.006	0.009	0.591	-	-0.378	0.690	0.598
SEB ImmoInvest	0.399	10	0.318	+	0.102	0.091	1.122	+	-0.001	0.002	-0.560	-	-0.077	0.157	0.632
UBS (D) Euroinv.	0.281	11	0.096	+	0.191	2.363	0.081	+	-0.017	0.009	-1.88*	-	0.218	3.861	0.956
UniImmo: D.	0.500	39	0.176	+	0.003	0.133	0.026	+	0.001	0.001	1.073	-	-0.157	0.165	0.346
WestInvest 1		NA		+				+				-			
WestInvest InterS.		NA		+				+				-			
Model: DMV ~ occupancy.rate+year.of.purchase+perc.ending.leases with DOCR < 0															
AXA IMMOS.		NA		+				+				-			
Deka-Immo.E.	0.876	2	-0.061	+	0.237	0.394	0.601	+	0.023	0.042	0.559	-	-1.177	3.111	0.742
Deka-ImmoFonds	0.002***	27	0.553	+	0.506	0.119	4.248***	+	-0.001	0.004	-0.203	-	0.012	0.223	0.958
grundbesitz-europa	0.020**	26	0.353	+	0.320	0.102	3.139***	+	-0.003	0.002	-1.665	-	0.110	0.084	0.203
HAUSINV. europa		NA		+				+				-			
SEB ImmoInvest	0.065	3	0.611	+	-0.035	0.161	-0.216	+	0.005	0.004	1.065	-	0.066	0.275	0.826
UBS (D) Euroinv.	0.997	1	-1.344	+	0.064	3.185	0.020	+	-0.010	0.465	-0.022	-	0.021	1.724	0.992
UniImmo: D.	0.590	7	0.300	+	0.183	0.185	0.985	+	0.002	0.003	0.680	-	-0.081	0.161	0.630
WestInvest 1		NA		+				+				-			
WestInvest InterS.		NA		+				+				-			

***, **, *, indicate statistical significance at the 0.01, 0.05 and 0.1 levels, respectively.

The most likely explanation for different mean value changes of properties by portfolio is that funds exerted an influence on the valuation of their properties in the year 2006. An alternative interpretation would disregard the assumption that all portfolios are fully diversified and resemble the German market sufficiently. In this case, different means of appraisals in 2006 between funds do not necessarily imply that funds influenced valuation in 2006, but the variance might be attributable to so far hidden characteristics of the funds' portfolios. According to IPD figures (section 2.3.2.1) on the correlation of German sub markets and use types, those differences seem not to be able to fully explain the observed valuation differences between portfolios.

The linear regression model to account for portfolio differences including the variables vacancy rate, date of purchase and percentage of ending leases is significant at the 0.05 level in 2006 for all portfolios with more than 20 properties and for most funds explains a big share of the variance in property value changes. The fact that the same model is far less significant and the explained variance is lower in 2005 and 2007 strengthens the argument that in fund crisis year 2006 many German properties were sold or were prepared for sale[22] and therefore valuations had to be adjusted to achievable market values, which is in line with the argument of the reluctance of institutional investors to adjust asset values in times of market depression[23]. The estimates of the three variables, especially the vacancy rate, differ largely by fund, which can be interpret such that different funds had to adjust property values of properties with high vacancy rates to a different extent in 2006. Only those variables differ significantly in 2006 compared to 2005 and 2007 that are derived within the valuation process such as the change in market value, the change in rental value and the change in the year's purchase. In contrast, the variables occupancy rate, change in occupancy rate and the percentage of ending leases, which are central input factors within the valuation process, do not change noticeably in 2006 (Table 2.7). This is further evidence that the valuation outcomes were different in 2006 but not the relevant market developments.

The results call for further research regarding the composition of the funds' portfolio characteristics to see whether the variance of value changes between the portfolios is attributable to so far hidden characteristics. But if the appraisal differences in 2006 do *not* stem from fund influence, the alternative explanation of undiversified portfolios bearing a significant degree of unsystematic risk is equally enlightening for investors being compensated only for the systematic risk of their investment.

---

22 By Investment Act (2008), German open-end funds are not allowed to sell properties below market values.

23 Several studies suggest that appraised values have been maintained despite declining markets (e.g Chinloy, Cho, & Megbolugbe, 1997; Geltner, 1993; Fisher, Geltner, & Webb, 1994; Hansz & Diaz, 2001; Hendershott & Kane, 1995). Graff and Young (1999) find random appraisal errors to be higher in times of market gridlock.

Consequences for the idiosyncratic risk of property portfolios (see literature review) are severe as well. The sharp increase of the cross-sectional standard deviation of property value changes in 2006 compared to 2005 and 2007 (Table 2.4) cannot be attributed to higher uncertainty in the valuation process regarding market developments, but is a direct consequence from different distributions of value changes depending on portfolio ownership. If a big proportion of cross-index return variance in property indices like the NPI index[24] for the US or the DIX[25] index for Germany stems from portfolio ownership, estimates derived from such indices may overstate the return variance within the single portfolios. Thus, to have a sufficiently diversified portfolio, much fewer properties might be needed as suggested by e.g. Young, Lee, and Devaney (2006).

The consequences of systematically biased appraisals, either biased by portfolio holding or biased by characteristics such as vacancy rates, are serious for the fixing of fund participation prices and on the aggregate level for direct property performance measurement. Autocorrelation in appraisal-based property indices has frequently been explained by the nature of the appraisal process, assuming that appraisers took previous appraisal values into consideration (see literature review). For the appraisals of German open-end fund properties in 2006, those model assumptions obviously did not hold as many portfolios were strongly devaluated in times of a rising market (yield compression). This means that neither the previous years' appraisals have been used as reference points, nor the current (and highly liquid) market transactions. A second assumption regarding the reliability of direct property indices is the notion that random appraisal errors will cancel out on portfolio level. If we interpret our results in such a way that in 2006 funds exerted an influence on property appraisals, appraisal errors are not random and thus will not cancel out on portfolio level.

Future research should use information on the fund level to explain appraisals of German open-end fund properties. It might be worth to investigate whether bond market returns and calendar anomalies in fund reporting months have an influence on the valuation of the fund's properties.

---

24 The National Council of Real Estate Investment Fiduciaries (NCREIF) publishes the NCREIF property index (NPI)

25 Deutscher Immobilien Index [German property index]

3 Lack of German real estate fund volatility - is the market or the valuer to blame?

3.1 Introduction

To the 31-12-2008, German open-end funds (GOEFs) hold only 29.9% of their property investments in Germany. European markets without Germany account for 58.1% of property market values and 11.9% are invested outside Europe. The biggest individual markets outside Germany are France with 19.0% and the UK with 9.9% property investment volume (BVI, 2009a). Intriguing is the contrast between the stable fund performances in times of worldwide financial turmoil and the developments on the mayor property markets the funds are invested in. The IPD OFIX-ALL[26] index for GOEFs shows to the 31-03-2009 a one-year return of 4.7% (IPD GmbH, 2009c). With respect to the German property market, fund returns are in line with property returns, as the IPD all property Total Return for Germany is 4.5% for 2008 (IPD GmbH, 2009a). With respect to their biggest foreign investment market France, stable fund returns are in contrast to property market developments The IPD France all property annual index shows a Total Return of -0.9%, and the biannual indicator shows -4.8% for only six month to the end of 2008. For the UK as the second biggest foreign investment market for GOEFs, the picture is even more puzzling: The IPD UK all property index for 2008 shows a Total Return of -22.1% (IPD, 2009b). As funds use financial leverage of up to 50% of their property values, fund returns are expected to fluctuate even more than the underlying property investments. The question arises why capital weighted returns of GOEFs that allocated about one third of their property values in France and the UK experienced hardly any return variations within the years of booming property markets (2005-2007) and bearish property markets (2007-2009)[27]?

As GOEFs are obliged by the Investment Act (2008) to publish market values of individual properties, we use an internationally unique dataset of 879 property values derived by external independent appraisal experts within the years 2004 to 2008. We compare valuations of properties held by GOEFs in Belgium, France, Italy, the Netherlands, Spain and the United Kingdom to mean valuation figures reported by IPD for the respective markets. We find significant differences with respect to changes in market values for all countries in almost all analysed years. With respect to the rental values however, findings are ambiguous. The most extreme valuation differences between GOEFs and the IPD data are found for the UK and France.

---

26 Offene Immobilien Fonds Index [Open-end property funds index]

27 Time spans overlap as the UK market showed a negative development already in 2007 while the French market turned negative in 2008.

3.2 Previous Research

When appraisals of comparable properties differ on portfolio level, a frequently stated assumption is that clients have influenced appraisers. The most relevant prior research has been presented as a working paper just recently by Crosby et al. at the ERES conference 2009. They investigate whether open-end funds in the UK influence appraisers in times of a market downturn to adjust values downwards more quickly. Crosby et al. (2009b) present a comprehensive review of client motivation to influence appraisers, possible means to exert influence and market circumstances where influence seems more likely. They argue that in the time of rapid property value decline in the UK in the second half of 2007, open-end funds in contrast to other market participants had a strong incentive to have their properties quickly marked down to market. They mention in this context that some fund managers switched to a fortnightly valuation frequency to ensure that capital redemptions were met at the current market value. The valuers on the other side were faced with much higher uncertainty for their appraisal values since the transaction volumes fell markedly. To empirically test their hypothesis, they use the IPD UK database and brake down quarterly performance data by fund type and find that the declines in capital values for open-end funds were significantly greater than for the remaining fund types and that the differences being most marked in the first half of 2007.

With respect to the German property market, there exists no research that compares individual property performance differentiated by investor type[28]. No research either exists on client influence on valuation, which internationally is a major research topic (Table 3.1). The majority of studies examine the US and UK market, while in recent times New Zealand, Nigeria and Taiwan / Singapore gained more attention. Due to confidentiality issues, most studies have an experimental setting, either theory building, with usually small sample sizes and in-depth interviews, or theory testing, with usually larger surveys. Almost all studies within the commercial sector find evidence on client influence on valuation, with respect to the residential market results are less clear.

For the **external characteristics**, the *definition of market value* has to be considered weakly defined, considering for example the idea of "sustainable" rental values (Downie et al., 1996), which results in a strong potential influence on valuers. For the remaining two factors *regulatory framework* and *market conditions* of the valuation industry we see no clear differences to e.g. the situation in the UK, although the valuation industry in Germany seems to be more diversified.

---

28 On fund level, Kurzrock, Gläsner, and Wilke (2009) compare returns of German open-end real estate retail funds with open-end specialist funds. Due to data limitations, the investigation does not address performance on the property level.

Table 3.1 Research on client influence on valuation

Author	Theory	Data	Property type	Country	Client influence?
Diaz (1990)	building	experiment	res.	US	yes
Diaz et al. (2002)	building	experiment	com.	UK,NZ	
Levy & Schuck (1999)	building	experiment	com.	NZ	yes
Levy & Schuck (2005)	building	experiment	com.	NZ	yes
Rushmore (1993)	building	theoretical	com.		yes
Smith (1986)	building	theoretical	com.		
Smolen (1994)	building	theoretical	com.		yes
Amidu & Aluko (2007)	testing	experiment	com.	NI	yes
Amidu, Aluko, & Hansz (2008)	testing	experiment	com.	NI	yes
Chen & Yu (2009)	testing	experiment	com.	TW,SI	yes
Cypher & Hansz (2003)	testing	experiment	com.	US	yes
Diaz & Hansz (2001)	testing	experiment	com.	US	yes
Diaz (1997)	testing	experiment	com.	US	
Gallimore & Wolverton (2000)	testing	experiment	com.	UK	yes
Havard (1999)	testing	experiment	ind.	UK	yes
Havard (2001)	testing	experiment	ind.	UK	yes
Kinnard et al. (1997)	testing	experiment	com.	US	yes
Smolen & Hambleton (1997)	testing	experiment	com.	US	yes
Spence & Thorson (1998)	testing	experiment	res.	US	
Wolverton & Gallimore (1999)	testing	experiment	com.	US	yes
Wolverton (2000)	testing	experiment	com.	US	yes
Worzala et al. (1998)	testing	experiment	res.	US	yes
Firoozi et al. (2006)	testing	private	res.	US	yes
Ferguson (1988)	testing	private	com.	US	yes

The **valuation characteristics** show most clearly that GOEFs are to be classified as potentially influencing valuers. For all four factors, the characteristics of GOEFs are likely to result in a strong influence on valuations. The *range of defensible values* is high, as the example of Deka-ImmobilienFonds in 2006 clearly proves. In a German property market characterised by strong yield compression and rather stable capital values of the properties of the other GOEFs, the German Deka-ImmobilienFonds portfolio comprising 129 properties was devalued by -18.8%[29]. The *amount of opinion* involved in appraisal of complex commercial properties is high, and the *valuation result* is highly important for fund management. A stable return development is crucial for the asset class of GOEFs, as return stability was the major sales argument over the last 50 years since the inception of the first fund, and the fragile capital structure due to the guaranteed daily participation redemption posts a risk of bank run in the case of a negative return development. As most funds are even considered as gilt-edged

29 As stated in the annual report of Deka-ImmobilienFonds in 2006, p. 23.

investments[30], a more volatile return development like e.g. in the case of US commingled real estate funds would not be acceptable. Finally, fund management has a high *incentive to influence valuations*. Remuneration of the investment firms is based on asset volume and in many cases on the fund performance. And, given a long bear market since the German reunification in 1990 and high capital influx over the entire period, we argue that steadily increasing fund volumes enabled fund management to bias appraisals upwards in times of poor market conditions with a high positive influence on fund returns and readjust values back again with a lower influence on fund returns given the than higher fund volumes.

Crosby (2009a) finds German rental value depreciation to vary significantly from other European markets. In this context, he presents a comprehensive review of research targeting valuation processes across Europe with a focus on Germany. The reviewed studies analyse characteristics of the valuation profession in the respective countries (McParland et al., 2002), the employed market value concepts (Downie et al., 1996) and IPD information on the performance measurement in the markets where they provide services in (IPD GmbH, 2007; IPD, 2008). Especially with respect to the rental value, he concludes that the German concept has elements of assuming sustainable values in contrast to market value concepts within the other countries.

Crosby attributes smoothing and lagging tendencies in German valuations to the industry's commitment to offer a product that has very low risk and volatility and to potential influence on the valuers. He argues that in Germany there exists no research on potential client influence on valuation[31], unlike in e.g. the US, UK or Australia and that Germany lies on a poor 12th rank on the Jones Lang LaSalle transparency index, behind a number of other European countries. Finally, Crosby concludes that: "[…] in a very long bear market, units priced by direct reference to valuations could become significantly overvalued, the situation which was perceived to exist in Germany." (Crosby 2007, p. 12).

Although research on German valuation practice is limited, it can be concluded that (1) client influence on appraisals is possible, internationally and in Germany, (2) the German valuation profession is in some regards different to the valuation profession of other countries and (3) GOEFs are an international particularity because the offer the least volatile fund returns.

---

30 German courts considered GOEFs in various decisions as gilt-edged investments. Among the sample of 15 analysed funds, all major funds and 11 funds in total have been considered gilt-edged by at least one decision (BVI, 2009b).

31 For example, Levy and Schuck (2005) extend earlier research (Levy & Schuck, 1999) and find evidence for New Zealand that clients exert influence on valuers by ways of expert and information power. Wolverton and Gallimore (1999) find for US appraisers that client feedback can have an influence on appraisals.

Table 3.2 Factors of client influence within GOEF valuation

	Factor	Strong potential influence on appraisers	High contingency to be influenced	Influence
Characteristics of the client	Size of client	big clients > strong influence	biggest portfolios by GAV in Europe	strong
	Type of client	mortgage lenders and agents influence more than other clients	no research for GOEFs	not clear
	Sophisticated vs. unsophisticated	sophisticated clients exert information power more successfully	sophisticated	strong
	Relationship with client	close relationship > strong influence	close, as few funds account for a big proportion of appraiser revenue	strong
External characteristics	Regulatory framework		no research on "margin of error" procedure in courts like in the UK	not clear
	Definition of value	well-defined definitions > weak influence	partly ambiguous (e.g. "sustainable" rents), central assumptions in WertV less transparent than in DCF approach	strong
	Market conditions of valuation industry	high competition > strong influence		not clear
Valuation characters tics	range of defensible values	high range > strong influence	high, especially in 2006, no changes of nominal values for more than 10% of German properties in 2006	strong
	Amount of opinion	managers of complex commercial properties have high amount of opinion > strong influence	GOEFs manage complex commercial properties	strong
	purpose of valuation	high importance of valuation result > strong influence	daily fixing of participation prices at NAV, potential of bank run, stable fund returns as central sales argument, considered as gilt-edged investment by German courts	strong
	Incentive to influence appraisal	high incentive > strong influence	remuneration performance-based, long bear market since German reunification, steady net capital influx over decades	strong

Source: own illustration, factors taken from Levy and Schuck (2005, p. 196).

All together, it seems possible that the market values of valuations assigned by GOEFs for properties abroad might differ significantly from the market values that were assigned by local market participants.

3.3 Research Design and Dataset

For the purpose of this paper the annual statements of accounts of 24 German open-end real estate retail funds have been analyzed. As the study focuses on value changes at the individual property level, only those reports could be included that provide appraisal data to the public domain on the individual property level. Only seven funds began to include individual property data into their reports as early as 2004. One year later, already 15 funds did so. From the year 2006 on, every fund presents the necessary data. As we want to include recent valuation data from foreign markets and use a homogeneous dataset with respect to the time period the appraisals took place, we limit the sample further to those funds that report to the months August to December, which are 15 out of 24 funds. Table 3.3 gives an overview of the funds' properties within the dataset. In total, 879 market values or appraisals of individual standing investment[32] properties from 2004 to 2008 are available for analysis. The aggregated market values of the portfolios range between 8.8 bn EUR in 2004 to 15.7 bn EUR in 2008.

Table 3.3 Properties of analyzed fund reports

	Sum MV in mill. EUR (number of properties)				
Country	**2004**	**2005**	**2006**	**2007**	**2008**
Belgium	386 (17)	444 (21)	1,252 (43)	1,198 (40)	1,015 (31)
France	2,352 (22)	3,537 (32)	4,904 (56)	5,567 (57)	5,566 (52)
Italy	209 (5)	616 (9)	1,351 (21)	1,490 (21)	1,619 (22)
Netherlands	975 (25)	1,086 (28)	2,003 (51)	2,356 (51)	2,115 (37)
Spain	852 (14)	901 (15)	1,375 (20)	1,300 (18)	1,419 (21)
UK	4,065 (29)	3,983 (29)	3,983 (31)	3,752 (28)	4,016 (33)
Total	8,839 (112)	10,568 (134)	14,868 (222)	15,663 (215)	15,749 (196)

For those properties which were part of the portfolios for two or more subsequent years and that were not under development within that time, the change in market value (DMV) is calculated:

$$DMV_{t1} = \frac{MV_{t1}}{MV_{t0}} - 1 \qquad (3.1)$$

Where DMV_{t1} denotes the percentage change in market values and MV_{t1} and MV_{t0} are the market values reported in two subsequent annual statements of accounts. As we are interested in the property appraisals rather than in aggregated property

32 As funds do not publish information regarding capital investments on the individual property level, properties that are qualified by the funds as being under development have been excluded.

performance on country level, we do not weight value changes by capital. This means that each property has the same influence on mean value changes within our dataset, regardless of its market value. The valuation figures reported by IPD are always capital weighted. As their sample size exceeds the number of observations of GOEFs by far, the influences of single properties one mean values are less severe[33]. All calculations refer to local currency, which is only relevant in the UK context, as all other analysed markets lie within the Euro zone. IPD figures stem from the IPD publications *IPD UK Quarterly Digest Q1 2009* (IPD, 2009a) and from the *IPD Multi National Index Spreadsheet 2008* (IPD, 2009b). We refer to the "all properties" segment published by IPD. An alternative would be to use the office segment as GOEFs primarily invest in office properties and retail properties. However, as the office segment has the highest weight in the IPD "all property" segment, figures do not differ strongly. The "all properties" segment resembles better the portfolios of GOEFs as the office or the retail segments do.

The problem when comparing GOEF valuations to IPD growth rates is that for both datasets the exact valuation dates are not available. Valuations of GOEFs occurred at some points of time within the reporting year. For eleven out of 15 funds in the chosen sample, the reporting year ends to September, for three funds to December and for one fund to August. Figure 3.1 illustrates the different time spans of the compared valuations for those funds that report to September. The upper part refers to countries where IPD publishes an annual index; the lower part refers to the UK, where also a quarterly index is available. The left bar next to the time bar indicates a twelve month period in which the first valuation took place, while the right bar indicates the period in which the second valuation took place. Both valuations are retrieved from different annual reports. The lower arrow connects the assumed average points of time of all valuations in both periods. Therefore, it is assumed that market values from an annual report to the 30.09.2007 occurred on average on the end of Q1 2007, and on the subsequent year on the end of Q1 2008. The procedure of valuing properties evenly distributed over the year is a particularity of GOEFs. IPD valuation figures for the annual index usually refer to the end of December. The consequence is that the assumed average valuation dates of GOEF lead the IPD valuation dates used for comparison by one quarter.

In the case of the UK (Figure 3.1, lower part), the match of the valuation dates is more precise as the IPD quarterly index of the respective first quarters is used for comparison.

33 However, if properties with high market values have different value changes than properties with low market values, this would induce a bias to the comparison. As IPD does not publish data on this issue, we cannot account for this thought-to-be minor bias.

Figure 3.1 Valuation periods of GOEFs and IPD

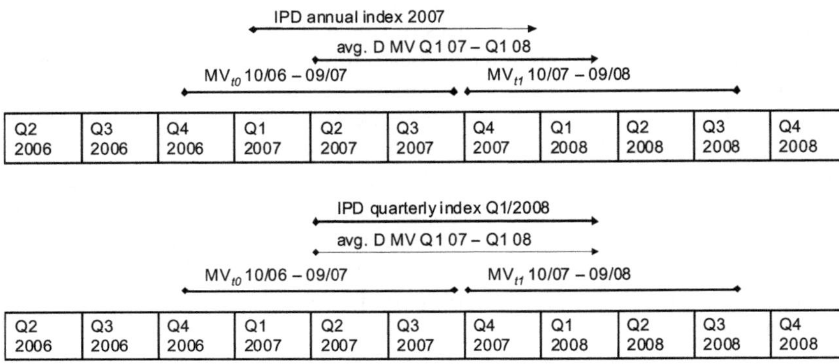

In the next section, we test the following hypothesis:

H1: Do mean value changes of GOEF properties differ significantly from mean value changes of properties within the IPD databank on the respective markets?

We employ a standard t-test to analyse whether differences in mean value changes are statistically significant. As IPD does not publish information on the variance of value changes, we assume that it is equal to the variance within our sample to conduct a two-sided t-test.

3.4 Results

3.4.1 Comparing capital growth and rental value growth

3.4.1.1 Capital growth rates of GOEF portfolios vs. locally held portfolios

Figure 3.2 presents histograms of capital value changes of GOEF properties in the UK as realised to the end of the first quarters 2005 to 2008. The solid lines within the histograms indicate the mean capital growth rate reported by the IPD UK quarterly index in the respective period (IPD, 2009a). It becomes evident at first glance that in times of rising markets (as reported by e.g. IPD) the IPD figures report much higher capital growth rates than the growth rates calculated for the individual GOEF properties. After the sharp market turn in Q1 2008, all capital growth rates of single properties of GOEFs are at least ten percentage points higher than the mean reported by IPD. Even without further statistical analyses it can be concluded that the capital growth rates of UK properties held by German funds differed between Q1 2005 to Q1 2008 from the IPD growth rates, and that the IPD rates show much more volatility.

Figure 3.2 Capital growth GOEFs vs. IPD UK Q1 2005 to Q1 2008

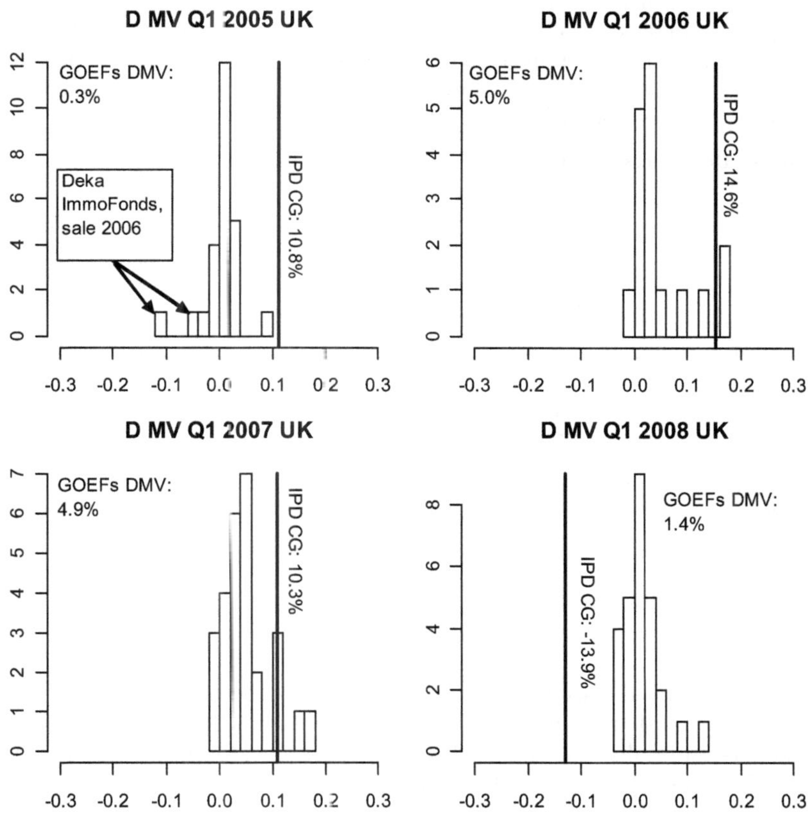

Interestingly, the most negative changes in capital values of GOEF properties do not fall into the Q1 2008 period, but were reported in the Q1 2005 period. The two properties with the most negative capital growth rates of -11.5% and -8.0% were sold in 2006 and are both part of the Deka-ImmobilienFonds portfolio. Although we cannot generalise from only two observation, a possible explanation for devaluing properties in a rising market may be the fact that GOEFs are prohibited by the Investment Act (2008) to sell off properties below the market value. The fact that Deka-ImmobilienFonds suffered a liquidity squeeze in that time and was supposedly forced to sell off properties may contribute to the explanation of those capital growth rates in contrast to IPD growth rates and also in contrast to capital growth rates of the other GOEFs properties.

Figure 3.3 illustrates the differences between GOEFs capital growth rates and IPD capital growth rates for all six analysed foreign investment markets. With the exception of UK results in the last period and Italy results in 2004 and 2006, all capital growth rates of GOEFs over all four periods are lower than IPD growth rates. In the case of the UK, the differences are most extreme with minus 10.5 percentage points difference within the 2004 period and plus 15.3 percentage points for the 2007 period. However, also French, Spanish and Dutch figures differ by more than five percentage points in the 2006 period.

Figure 3.3 Differences in capital growth rates of GOEFs vs. IPD

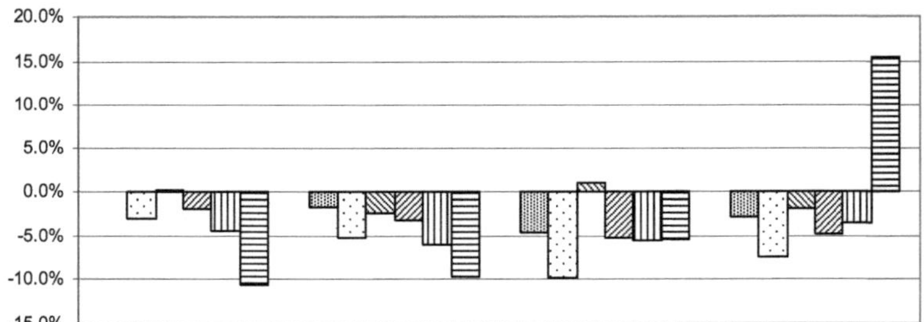

	2004	2005	2006	2007
Belgium		-1.8%	-4.5%	-2.8%
France	-3.0%	-5.2%	-9.8%	-7.4%
Italy	0.2%	-2.4%	0.9%	-1.8%
Netherlands	-1.9%	-3.1%	-5.1%	-4.7%
Spain	-4.5%	-5.9%	-5.6%	-3.4%
UK	-10.5%	-9.6%	-5.4%	15.3%

Table 3.4 presents the results of the t-tests to compare mean capital growth rates of GOEFs against the capital growth rates reported by IPD in the respective markets.T-test results show at the 0.05 significance level for the markets France, the Netherlands, Spain and the UK in all four analysis periods that mean value changes of GOEF properties differed from IPD capital growth figures. For the remaining two markets, results reach significance only in 2007 (Italy) or 2006 and 2007 in the case of Belgium . As the true variances within the IPD samples are not known and the Shapiro-Wilk tests (SW) reject normality for the majority of the distributions of GOEFs property value changes, t-test results have to be interpret cautiously.

We also applied a bootstrapping algorithm to compare the means of both populations. Following Lunneborg (2000), we restrict analysis to those cases where the number of observations is at least 25.

Table 3.4 Change in market values t-test results by country and year

			2004	2005	2006	2007
Belgium		*IPD CG*		*0.4%*	*2.8%*	*3.8%*
	GOEFs DMV	N	16	21	39	30
		Mean	-2.6%	-1.4%	-1.7%	0.9%
		Median	-1.0%	-0.4%	-0.1%	0.9%
		Sd	3.7%	6.6%	5.5%	6.4%
		SW-test		0.164	**0.000**	0.123
		t-test		0.234	**0.000**	**0.021**
France		*IPD CG*	*3.6%*	*8.8%*	*15.4%*	*11.8%*
	GOEFs DMV	N	22	27	51	52
		Mean	0.5%	3.6%	5.6%	4.4%
		Median	0.7%	2.5%	4.9%	4.8%
		Sd	1.9%	6.0%	5.7%	5.4%
		SW-test	0.171	**0.005**	**0.037**	**0.000**
		t-test	**0.000**	**0.000**	**0.000**	**0.000**
Italy		*IPD CG*	*2.2%*	*2.7%*	*2.6%*	*3.8%*
	GOEFs DMV	N	5	8	17	20
		Mean	2.4%	0.3%	3.6%	2.0%
		Median	0.7%	-0.3%	2.3%	1.3%
		Sd	8.0%	7.3%	4.7%	2.3%
		SW-test	0.200	**0.040**	**0.016**	**0.030**
		t-test	0.964	0.388	0.432	**0.003**
Netherlands		*IPD CG*	*1.7%*	*4.1%*	*6.6%*	*5.8%*
	GOEFs DMV	N	25	20	46	33
		Mean	-0.2%	1.1%	1.5%	1.1%
		Median	0.0%	0.7%	1.0%	0.2%
		Sd	3.6%	5.9%	4.1%	3.5%
		SW-test	**0.000**	0.233	**0.000**	**0.001**
		t-test	**0.015**	**0.027**	**0.000**	**0.000**
Spain		*IPD CG*	*5.0%*	*10.6%*	*11.3%*	*7.7%*
	GOEFs DMV	N	14	12	17	17
		Mean	0.5%	4.6%	5.8%	4.3%
		Median	0.2%	3.2%	4.3%	4.1%
		Sd	4.1%	7.8%	5.8%	3.1%
		SW-test	0.198	0.823	**0.046**	0.850
		t-test	**0.001**	**0.023**	**0.001**	**0.043**
			Q1 05	Q1 06	Q1 07	Q1 08
UK		*IPD CG*	*10.8%*	*14.6%*	*10.3%*	*-13.9%*
	GOEFs DMV	N	25	17	27	27
		Mean	0.3%	5.0%	4.9%	1.4%
		Median	0.4%	3.1%	4.1%	0.6%
		Sd	3.5%	5.6%	4.4%	3.8%
		SW-test	**0.000**	**0.001**	**0.007**	**0.004**
		t-test	**0.000**	**0.000**	**0.000**	**0.000**

bold figures indicate significance at the 0.05 level

After bootstrapping the data 10,000 times, the means of changes in market values differ significantly at the 0.001 level for all countries in all periods with 25 or more observations. The results of the non-parametric bootstrap confirm t-test results[34].

3.4.1.2 Rental value growth of GOEF portfolios vs. locally held portfolios

While Crosby (2009b) found that UK open-end funds mark down to market more quickly than other UK market participants do and in some cases even switch to fortnightly appraisals to be able to reimburse participations at market value, this behaviour is certainly not true for German open-end funds and their investments in the UK. Crosby (2009a) argued that different appraisal results of German appraisers may be explained by a rent concept that is rather oriented on a sustainable value than on actual market values. We will test his proposition by comparing the change in estimated rental values (DERV) of GOEF properties to IPD's figures on rental value growth. The change of estimated rental values is calculated analogously to the change in market values:

$$DERV_{t1} = \frac{ERV_{t1}}{ERV_{t0}} - 1 \qquad (3.2)$$

Where ERV_{t1} denotes the change or delta in estimated rental values and ERV_{t1} and ERV_{t0} are the estimated rental values reported in two subsequent annual statements of accounts. We will test the following hypothesis:

H2: Do mean changes in estimated rental values of GOEF properties differ significantly from the rental value growth of properties within the IPD databank on the respective markets?

Figure 3.4 presents histograms of estimated rental value changes of GOEF properties in the UK as realised to the end of the first quarters 2005 to 2008. The solid lines within the histograms indicate the rental value growth rate reported by the IPD UK quarterly index in the respective periods. Unlike in the case of changes in market values (Figure 3.2), the IPD mean rental value growth lies within the distribution of GOEFs estimated rental value changes. The average difference over the four periods of figures reported by IPD versus mean rental value changes of GOEFs is 1.8 percentage points, while it is 10.2 percentage points for changes in market values. Also striking is the fact that in the time of IPD reported market downturn in period Q1 2008 both sources report positive

34 A frequently raised criticism on bootstrap approaches is that error prone data and biased samples are being repeated by the resampling. If data quality is poor, classic parametric approaches however face the same problem (Rodgers, 1999). In case of the presented paper, our sample consists of 15 out of 24 GOEFs, which is more than half of the entire population.

changes in rental values, in case of the GOEFs even higher rental growth rates than in the period Q1 2007. With respect to the UK, it can be concluded that the higher volatility of IPD capital growth rates in contrast to GOEF changes in market value does not stem from rental value assumptions but is attributable to changes in the capitalization rates.

Table 3.5 shows the results of the t-tests to compare mean rental value changes of GOEF properties to the IPD rental growth figures by country and year. In contrast to the changes in market values (Table 3.4) for which significant differences were found for all countries with only three periods in Italy and Belgium where results did not reach significance, in the case of rental value changes significant differences are the exception. For Belgium, France and Italy, there are no significant differences within all four periods. For Spain, the analysis could not be conducted, as IPD does not report rental value growth rates for this country. In the case of the Netherlands and the UK, mean rental value changes differ in only two of four periods each, in the remaining periods means are not distinguishable statistically.

We again applied a bootstrapping algorithm to compare the means of both populations for those cases where at least 25 observations are available. After bootstrapping the data 10,000 times, the means of the rental value changes differ significantly at the 0.001 level for all countries in all periods. The fact that under the bootstrapping approach even minor differences of rental value changes as for example in the case of Belgium in 2006 become significant, questions the appropriateness of the approach. In the example, the mean rental value change reported by IPD is -0.93%, while it is -1.04% in the GOEF population. Even if we assumed that those differences are significant given only 33 observations, the minimal strength of the effect deems this result of minor economic relevance. As parametric t-test results are not significant in cases of minor mean differences (e.g. Belgium 2006, the Netherlands 2004 and 2005), we consider those results superior in the given context.

As argued with respect to the UK, it can be concluded that given more similar (though in many cases not identical) valuer assumptions on rental value changes for GOEF properties and IPD sample properties and at the same time significant and substantial differences with respect to changes in market values, the more volatile market values of the IPD sample stem from the assumption of more volatile capitalization rates.

3.4.2 Constituents of the capital growth

After results have shown that the valuations of GOEF properties differ primarily with regard to the capitalization rates assumptions from the valuations of the local property owners, the analysis deepens explicitly into the constituents of market values, namely the already mentioned change in estimated rental value (DERV) and the change in the year's purchase (DYP).

Figure 3.4 Rental value growth GOEFs vs. IPD UK Q1 2005 to Q1 2008

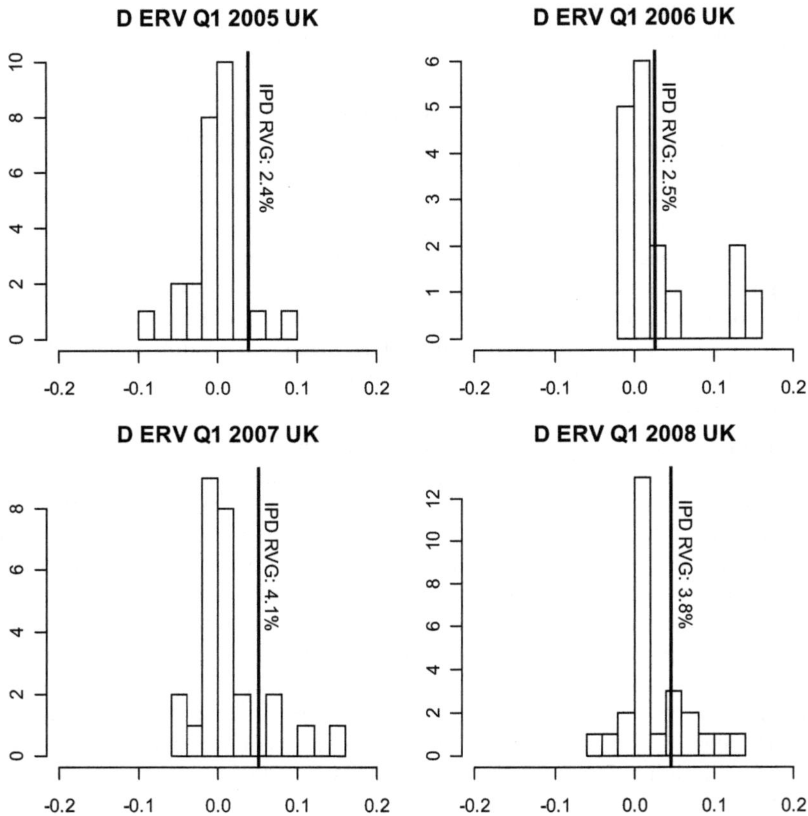

While the market values and the estimated rental values could be directly retrieved from the funds' statements of accounts, the year's purchase, or the rent multiplier, has to be calculated:

$$YP = \frac{MV}{ERV} \tag{3.3}$$

MV stands for the market value and *ERV* for the estimated rental value.

Table 3.5 Change in estimated rental values t-test results by country and year

Country			2004	2005	2006	2007
Belgium		*IPD RVG*			-0.9%	-0.1%
	GOEFs DERV	N	13	16	33	24
		Mean	-2.8%	-2.9%	-1.0%	-0.5%
		Median	0.0%	-0.6%	0.0%	0.0%
		Sd	4.0%	3.9%	3.2%	3.9%
		SW-test		**0.002**	**0.005**	**0.030**
		t-test			0.853	0.693
France		*IPD RVG*	0.8%	1.2%	3.0%	4.3%
	GOEFs DERV	N	22	27	45	47
		Mean	0.2%	-0.4%	2.5%	3.3%
		Median	0.0%	0.0%	1.7%	2.8%
		Sd	2.8%	5.8%	4.7%	4.1%
		SW-test	**0.049**	0.079	**0.012**	**0.000**
		t-test	0.336	0.147	0.479	0.106
Italy		*IPD RVG*	2.9%	1.9%	2.9%	2.4%
	GOEFs DERV	N	5	7	17	19
		Mean	3.3%	-0.6%	2.6%	2.0%
		Median	0.0%	0.4%	1.2%	1.4%
		Sd	7.3%	4.8%	4.1%	3.5%
		SW-test	0.059	**0.005**	**0.000**	**0.002**
		t-test	0.901	0.207	0.798	0.619
Netherlands		*IPD RVG*	1.2%	0.9%	1.9%	2.7%
	GOEFs DERV	N	25	20	46	33
		Mean	1.3%	1.1%	0.1%	0.4%
		Median	0.8%	0.8%	0.0%	0.0%
		Sd	3.4%	3.7%	3.9%	2.7%
		SW-test	**0.001**	0.147	**0.000**	**0.009**
		t-test	0.957	0.806	**0.004**	**0.000**
Spain		*IPD RVG*	n.a.	n.a.	n.a.	n.a.
	GOEFs DERV	N	14	12	15	16
		Mean	1.8%	1.8%	3.3%	3.8%
		Median	0.3%	3.3%	2.7%	3.1%
		Sd	6.1%	5.2%	3.5%	4.1%
		SW-test				
		t-test				
			Q1 05	Q1 06	Q1 07	Q1 08
UK		*IPD RVG*	2.4%	2.5%	4.1%	3.8%
	GOEFs DERV	N	25	17	26	26
		Mean	-0.4%	3.1%	1.4%	2.5%
		Median	-0.1%	0.2%	0.4%	1.2%
		Sd	3.2%	5.6%	4.2%	4.2%
		SW-test	**0.004**	**0.000**	**0.000**	**0.010**
		t-test	**0.000**	0.701	**0.003**	0.144

bold figures indicate significance at the 0.05 level

Analogously to the calculation of the change in market values and the change in estimated rental values, the change in the year's purchase (DYP) is calculated as follows:

$$DYP = \frac{YP_{t1}}{YP_{t0}} - 1 \qquad (3.4)$$

With YP_{t1} denoting the year's purchase at t_1 and YP_{t0} denoting the year's purchase at t_0. Table 3.6 shows the changes in market values and their constituents[35], the change in estimated rental values and the change in the rent multiplier. For most of the countries in most of the periods, the constituents move in the same direction, even though not always in the same extent. Only in the case of the Netherlands and Spain in 2004 there is a converging pattern, with rising rental values being offset by decreasing multiplier values.

Table 3.6 Capital growth attributed to rental value and year's purchase

	Mean	**2004**	**2005**	**2006**	**2007**
Belgium	DCG	-2.6%	-1.4%	-1.7%	0.9%
	DERV	-2.8%	-2.9%	-1.0%	-0.5%
	DYP	-0.7%	-0.1%	-1.1%	0.4%
France	DCG	0.5%	3.6%	5.6%	4.4%
	DERV	0.2%	-0.4%	2.5%	3.3%
	DYP	0.4%	4.3%	3.3%	1.5%
Italy	DCG	2.4%	0.3%	3.6%	2.0%
	DERV	3.3%	-0.6%	2.6%	2.0%
	DYP	-0.9%	2.2%	1.0%	0.1%
Netherlands	DCG	-0.2%	1.1%	1.5%	1.1%
	DERV	1.3%	1.1%	0.1%	0.4%
	DYP	-1.4%	-0.1%	1.4%	0.4%
Spain	DCG	0.5%	4.6%	5.8%	4.3%
	DERV	1.8%	1.8%	3.3%	3.8%
	DYP	-1.1%	2.8%	2.1%	0.4%
		Q1 05	**Q1 06**	**Q1 07**	**Q1 08**
UK	DCG	0.3%	5.0%	4.9%	1.4%
	DERV	-0.4%	3.1%	1.4%	2.5%
	DYP	0.7%	1.9%	3.6%	-0.9%

On the aggregated level over all properties, the changes in estimated rental values and the yield changes show with the mentioned exceptions in 2004 no surprising patterns. Broken down on the individual property level however, the negative correlation of the change in estimated rental value and the change in the year's purchase is surprising (Figure 3.5). For all four periods, the correlation is negative at the 0.01 significance level, with coefficients ranging between -0.384 in 2004 and -0.237 in 2007.

Figure 3.6 illustrates the unexpected valuation pattern in more detail using only UK properties and dividing the sample by years. The solid line is the linear re-

35 For the periods 2006 and 2007, the constituents add up (with minor inaccuracy due to the multiplicative relation and rounding errors), but for the periods 2004 and 2005, the sample of the observations differ. In the earlier two periods, all funds published information on market values (to calculate DMV), but not all did so for the estimated rental values (to calculate DERV and YP). For those periods, the figures do not always add up.

gression line[36]. For all four years, the slope is negative, which could be interpret as a result of properties that maintained their market values while having their constituents, rental values and multipliers, changed in an offsetting way. For the majority of the countries and years, results are quiet similar to the UK example. Splitting up the sample by fund reveals that the negative correlation of the two constituents of the change in market value is not prevalent within all funds.

Figure 3.5 Change in rental value vs. change in year's purchase, all markets

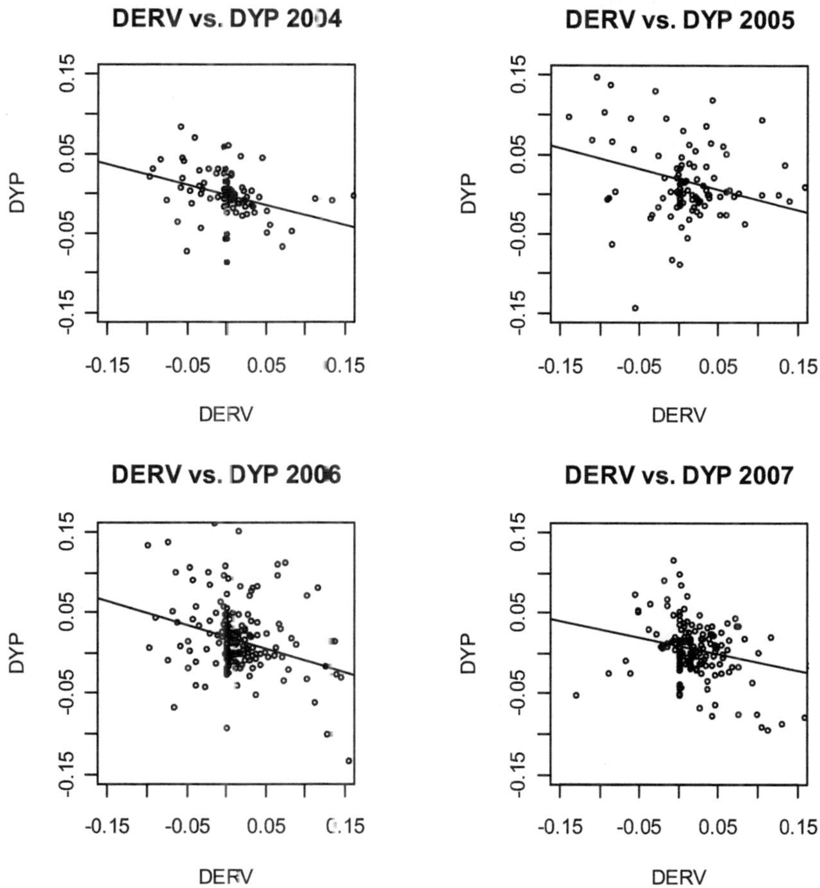

---

36 For 2004, the regression misses significance with a p-value of 0.228 and only 25 observations. For 2005, the regression neither is significant (p-value 0.288, n=17). For 2006 and 2007 results are significant at the 0.01 level (p-values 0.001 and 0.002, n=26 and n=26).

Table 3.7 shows that for six out of 15 funds the correlation coefficients are significantly negative at the 0.05 level. For some funds, the coefficients miss significance due to the limited observation number. The fact that the correlation is not significant for Deka-ImmobilienEuropa with 140 observations shows that valuation is different with regard to the constituents of the change in market values by fund. Interestingly, all other three Deka Bank funds, namely Deka-ImmobilienGlobal, Deka-ImmobilienFonds and WestInvest 1 neither show significant correlation coefficients, which could be interpret such that valuation differences might also stem from the investment firm rather than from the fund itself.

Figure 3.6 Change in rental value vs. change in year's purchase, UK market

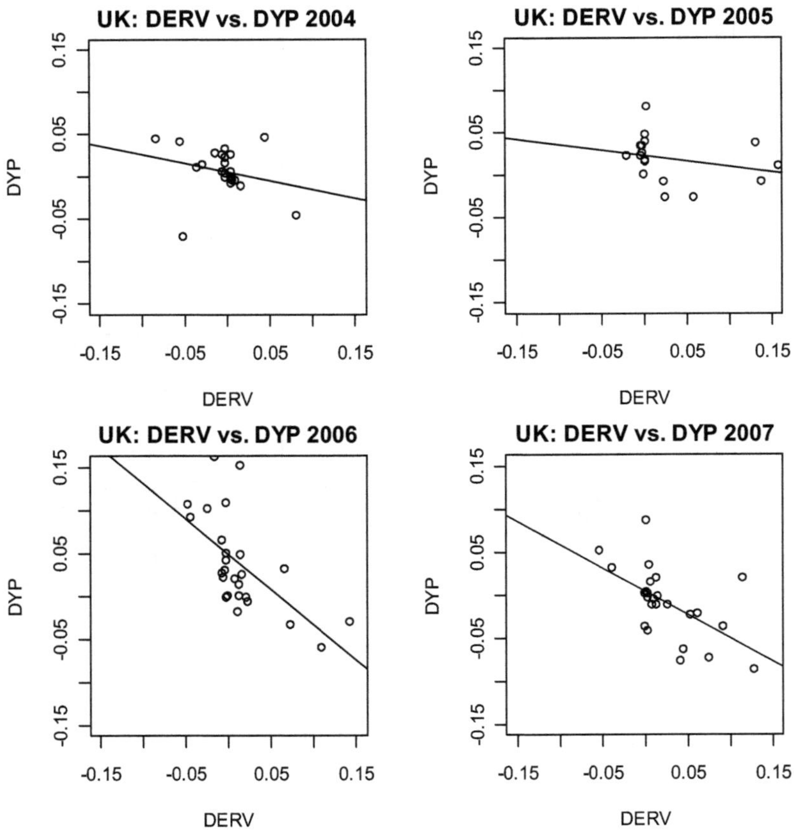

3.4.3 Quantile regression of rent multiplier

The results show a significant negative correlation of the change in rental values and the change in the rent multiplier or year's purchase. The effect is stable over all four years of analysis and all six markets. With regard to portfolio holding, the effect is significant for only six out of 15 funds. To further check the robustness of the results, we employ a quantile regression approach (Koenker & Basset, 1978) to test whether the correlation is equally significant at several points of the distribution. At this stage, it is important to define which of the two variables is considered the independent one (Heckman, 1979; Koenker & Hallock, 2001). Figure 3.7 illustrates the correlations on fund level for the three funds with the highest numbers of observation and for UniImmo: Europa, as for this fund the correlation coefficient is close to minus one.

Table 3.7 Correlation of DERV and DYP between 2004 and 2007 by funds

Fund	Df	p-value	Estimate
CS EUROREAL (A) EUR	72	**0.000**	-0.506
DEGI EUROPA	9	0.127	-0.489
DEGI INTERNATIONAL	24	**0.005**	-0.533
Deka-ImmobilienEuropa	140	0.439	-0.065
Deka-ImmobilienGlobal	40	0.765	-0.047
Deka-ImmobilienFonds	29	0.660	0.082
EURO ImmoProfil	3	0.888	-0.088
grundbesitz-europa	87	**0.006**	-0.290
HANSAimmobilia	18	0.813	-0.056
HAUS-INVEST global	2	-	-
INTER ImmoProfil	20	0.507	0.149
TMW Immo. Weltfonds	9	**0.017**	-0.696
UBS (D) EUROINVEST	39	**0.000**	-0.582
UniImmo: Europa	20	**0.000**	-0.895
WestInvest 1	42	0.539	-0.095

bold figures indicates significance at the 0.05 level

The case of UniImmo: Europa highlights the supposedly prevalent valuation pattern. Many properties hardly change with respect to the market value, but the factors estimated rental value and year's purchase do so. In case of the two properties in the upper left corner, the amount to which rental values and multipliers are interchanged is surprising. While the market values of the two properties remain almost constant (+1.75% and +1.65%), their multipliers go down by 13.30% and 7.48% while their estimated rental values increase by 17.36% and 9.86%. Within the valuation process, the appraiser defines the market value and the rental value, whereas the year's purchase or rent multiplier is only calculated in the context of this paper but is not reported in the GOEFs' statements of accounts. Without further assumptions on appraiser behaviour, we cannot decide whether the empirically observed negative correlation of rental change and change in the rent multiplier is an effect of the (given) change in rental value on the (dependent) market value or vice versa. In the first case, the underlying argument would be that the valuer wants to (or has to) change the rental value and does not want to adjust the market value linearly, as it would be the case if the rent multiplier remained unchanged. In the second case, the valuer wants to (or has to) change the market value, but does not want to adjust the rental value accordingly. If we merely aim at explaining smoothed property value changes, the direction of the causality is not important, as both described relations lead to smoothed changes in market values in comparison the changes of the rental values and rent multipliers. For the correct specification of the quantile regression however, we need to identify the nature of the relation. Fortunately, a brief comparison of the histograms of the change in market values (Figure 3.2) and the change in rental values (Figure 3.6) shows that rental value changes are rather in line with the development reported by the local market participants, while the changes in market values and therefore the change in the rent multipliers differ extremely.

We therefore argue that the change in rental values has to be considered the independent variable, as given by the market. The change of the rent multiplier (DYP) is considered the dependent variable, as it is certainly not given (if even influenced) by market developments as described by the local participants. We compute a linear parametric quantile regression on a set of quantiles, in particular the 20th, 40th, 60th, and 80th quantiles. For comparison, we also report the Ordinary Least Squares (OLS) results of the regression:

$$DYP \sim DERV + \varepsilon \tag{3.5}$$

Where DYP denotes the change in the rent multiplier, $DERV$ stands for the change in rental value, and ε is the error term. Table 3.8 reports the results of the quantile regression using the change of the rent multiplier as the independent variable. The last column shows ordinary OLS regression results. For all quantiles, significance exceeds the 0.001 level and all regression slopes are negative. The steepest slopes however are found in the extreme ends of the distribution, namely the 20th and 80th percentiles.

We interpret results such as changes in rental values did not influence changes in market values in the anticipated linear relation in the years 2004 to 2007. The negative correlation of the change in rental value and the change in the rent multiplier results in less volatility of the change of market values than the volatility of the individual components would suggest. The arguable smoothing of property value changes via the rent multiplier is stronger in cases of extreme negative rental value changes (20th percentile) and in cases of extreme positive rental value changes (80th percentile) as compared to moderate levels of rental value changes (40th and 60th percentiles).

Figure 3.7 Correlation of DERV and DYP by funds

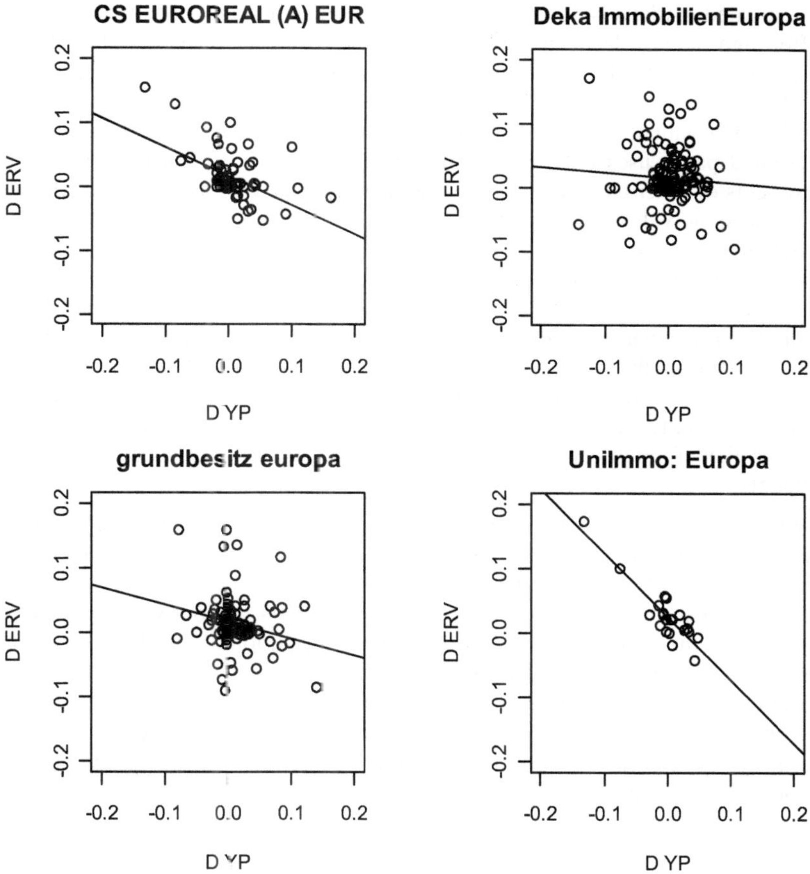

Table 3.8 Quantile regression of change in rent multiplier

	τ = 20	τ = 40	τ = 60	τ = 80	OLS
Constant					
Estimate	-0.010***	0.000	0.013***	0.036***	0.013***
Std. error	0.002	0.001	0.002	0.003	0.002
t value	-5.916	0.101	6.631	12.209	6.940
DERV					
Estimate	-0.187***	-0.127***	-0.156***	-0.238***	-0.247***
Std. error	0.039	0.016	0.020	0.059	0.039
t value	-4.804	-7.794	-7.950	-4.046	-6.349

***, **, *, indicate statistical significance at the 0.01, 0.05 and 0.1 levels, respectively.

3.5 Results

Our main findings are that the valuation results of GOEF properties in all the investigated markets Belgium, France, Italy, the Netherlands, Spain and the UK differ significantly from the valuations of the local market participants in the respective markets. Those findings are not in contrast to the findings of Crosby et al. (2009b) that state that open-end funds in the UK influence appraisers to mark down valuations more quickly in times of a bearish market, because the presented paper uses only foreign investments of GOEFs, but not foreign investments of other German-based market participants. But, as GOEFs could employ the same valuers as UK open-end funds to appraise their UK properties, it is evident from the results that they do not opt for this alternative. It can be concluded that the management of GOEFs in contrast to their UK colleagues is not interested in quickly marking down asset values in times of market crisis. Especially when comparing GOEFs capital growth rates from Q1 2005 to Q1 2008 to IPD capital growth, a substantial smoothing effect is found. While the change in rental values is at least similar within GOEFs compared to IPD figures, the yield shift differs extremely. German open-end funds do not change the capitalization rates of their foreign investments in a comparable way to the local market participants.

A further and unexpected valuation patter was found: The negative relation between the rental value change and the rent multiplier, with the consequence of smoother property value changes than the volatility of the rental value would suggest. Results are robust for all six analysed markets, all four years of analysis and also for the four analysed quantiles of the distribution of the change in rental value. With respect to the analysed portfolios, the effect is significant only for six out of 15 portfolios. The negative correlation of the rental value change and the change of the rent multiplier has the effect that changes in rental value are not fully reflected in changes of the market value, which again partly explains smoothed value changes of properties held by German open-end funds.

4 Keep the Faith? - Return Stability of Open-end Real Estate Funds

4.1 Introduction

Returns of German open-end real estate retail funds have shown a remarkably stable development over the last decades. The annualized standard deviations of returns of GOEFs with more than ten years return history is for nine out of 13 funds below one percent on average over the last ten years. Three funds realized standard deviations close to one percent, and only one fund showed more volatile returns with a standard deviation of 2.18%. Those thirteen funds make up the IPD OFIX-10 index which realized an annual volatility of 0.52% between 1999 and 2008 (IPD GmbH, 2009a). From an international perspective, annualised volatilities of monthly fund returns of one percent are exceptionally low. Using data of two commingled real estate funds (CREF) in the US, Brueggemann et al. (1992) report annualised volatilities of 5.7% and 6.2% between 1972 and 1989. Gallo, Lockwood, and Rodriguez (2006) examine 65 pension CREFs in the US during 1985 to 2002 of which 23 funds are open-end. Annualised standard deviations of individual fund returns ranged between 1.87% and 13.40%. The index of 23 open-end CREFs shows a standard deviation of 2.76%.

Mueller et al. (2008) analysed monthly returns from listed property companies and Real Estate Investment Trusts (REIT) in the US and the EU from 1987 to 2005. They built portfolios of all listed companies and classified times of low volatility on the index level when volatilities ranged between 1.5% and 3.9%. Even in times of low market volatility, the volatility on the diversified index level is several times higher than the volatilities of the individual German open-end funds. Stevenson (2000) presents similarly high volatilities of returns for an international sample of listed real estate funds between 1980 and 1997.

The German fund managers explain the low volatility of participation prices with stable cash flows of long lease contracts and diversification benefits from investments in different property markets. However, it is in the self interest of fund management to signal stable fund returns in order to indicate a low investment risk to the investor. Since investment risk of property funds is usually measured in terms of monthly or quarterly standard deviation of fund returns, the fund management can try to avoid significant return deviations within the year to attain a good ranking position with respect to performance measures like the Sharpe Ratio. As fund returns are calculated based on the value of fund participations which are not traded on an exchange but directly reflect fund's net asset values, timely and accurate information on the value changes of fund properties is crucial to calculate fund returns. The presence of Sharpe Ratios in excess of 2 given annualized excess returns between only 1.4% and 1.8% for two major funds[37] between 1999 and 2008 raise the question whether the underlying asset volatility is correctly reflected in monthly fund return deviations.

German real estate funds in the international context

While for European listed real estate funds there exists quiet a substantial amount of studies[38] addressing performance characteristics and the relations to other asset classes such as stocks and bonds, the body of literature on non-listed European real estate funds is fairly limited. Brounen et al. (2007) present an overview of all European non-listed real estate funds, but they do not report fund returns and volatility. They argue that a lack of information transparency was a major problem for investors in the past and that performance information is still very limited in Europe. With respect to the majority of their sample of 481 funds, this contention is true. For the subset of German open-end retail funds however, it is not. We argue that the degree of transparency of German open-end retail funds is among the highest of all property vehicles worldwide, listed and non-listed. Information of fund returns on a monthly basis is easily available, and as a consequence of the German Investment Act (2008), all funds publish market values of single properties every year since 2006[39]. Although the group of German open-end retail funds (as opposed to funds targeting institutional investors) comprises only 24 funds, aggregated gross asset value (GAV) amounts to 76.6 bn. EUR by the end of 2006, which is about 23% of total gross asset value of all 481 European non-listed funds, and even 32% of the GAV of those 275 funds classified as core investment style (Brounen et al., 2007).

Given the size of the industry, research on German open-end funds is fairly limited in general.

Bannier et al. (2008) provide a comprehensive analysis based on banking theory on German open-end funds. They bring forward the idea of Fama and Jensen (1983) to the German funds that a fragile fund structure can serve as a disciplining device to detain management from moral hazard and present an explanation why open-end funds have remained successful only in Germany. Maurer et al. (2004) compare the return distribution of direct property investments between Germany, the UK and the US. They construct an index to measure German property performance based on fund returns of German open-end real estate funds and find autocorrelation of quarterly property returns to be significant for

37 The two open-end funds with the highest returns from 1999 to 2008, SEB ImmoInvest and CS EUROREAL (A) EUR, with annualised excess returns of 1.40% and 1.74% over EURIBOR, achieved Sharpe Ratios of 3.18 and 2.83 given their extremely low return volatility of 0.62% and 0.44%.

38 See e.g. Brounen and Eichholz (2003), Brounen and Ter Laak (2005), Conover, Friday, and Sirmans (2002), and Gordon, Canter, and Webb (1998).

39 However, this data is not easily available for research, as no central databank comprising those values exists. The data analysed in this paper has been collected from 69 individual statements of accounts.

one to four quarters lag. Assuming the appraisal process as the source of autocorrelation and non-normality[40] of fund returns, they unsmooth property returns. The unsmoothed return series for Germany is six times more volatile than the original series.

Research on smoothed property returns

There exists no research on the issue of *timing* of property valuations resulting in smoothed fund returns, but the issue of return smoothing itself has been subject to many studies. A prominent line of research addresses property valuation and its consequences on direct property performance measurement on the index level. In one of the most influential studies on direct real estate performance measurement, Geltner (1989a) presents a theory of **smoothing of real estate appraisals** and suggests a methodology to unsmooth property returns on the index level to reveal "real" asset volatility. He argues that two levels of smoothing can enter property index returns: Firstly, at the disaggregate level of individual property appraisals over time and secondly at the aggregate index level. He refers to the first level of smoothing as "lack of confidence" and argues that the appraiser cannot be certain if his current estimate of market value meets exactly the true market value. He argues that given market value estimates of the same property for the previous year (as it is usually the case for commingled real estate funds), appraisers will consider the previous year's estimate to at least some extent. Many subsequent studies (e.g. De Wit, 1993; Fisher, Geltner, & Webb, 1994; Geltner, 1993; Quan & Quigley, 1991) build on Geltner's framework and refine his suggestion to "unsmooth" returns to derive the "true" direct real estate return. Corgel and deRoss (1999) show that different assumptions regarding the appraisal process and thus different models to unsmooth returns can result in very different real estate weights of an optimal multi asset portfolio. As Geltner's unsmoothing methodology relies heavily on assumptions regarding appraisal behaviour, Lai and Wang (1998) question those assumptions[41] and present scenarios in which appraisal-based time series can exhibit even *more* volatility than true asset volatility, and state that: "It is unreasonable to conclude that something is wrong with appraisers just because we observe that the variance of appraisal-based returns seems artificially low." (p. 532). Their contradicting argumentation is interesting, because for German open-end funds, there exist the same return patterns (i.e. low volatility and autocorrelation) that initiated the attempts to unsmooth returns, but in the presented paper it can be shown that at

---

40 Also internationally, many studies on return distribution of real estate funds have found that return distributions lack normality (e.g. Byrne & Lee, 1997; Myer & Webb, 1994; Young, 2008; Young & Graff, 1995). With respect to German open-end real estate funds Maurer et al. (2004) and Benk et al. (2008) confirm those findings.

41 Geltner, MacGregor, and Schwann (2003) concede that Lai and Wang (1998) raised a valid point in that smoothing literature had simply started from the assumption that smoothing existed. However, they do not agree upon their further argumentation.

least for German open-end funds, the assumed influence of individual property value changes is not the cause for the observed serial correlation in fund returns.

Although primarily based on anecdotal evidence, the probably most straight forward investigation on potential influence on property valuation by German open-end funds is presented by Crosby (2007). Crosby attributes smoothing and lagging tendencies in German valuations to the industry's commitment to offer a product that has very low risk and volatility and to potential influence on the valuers. He argues that in Germany there exists no research on potential client influence on valuation[42], unlike in e.g. the US, UK or Australia and that Germany lies on a poor 12th rank on the Jones Lang LaSalle transparency index, behind a number of other European countries. Finally, he concludes that: "[...] in a very long bear market, units priced by direct reference to valuations could become significantly overvalued, the situation which was perceived to exist in Germany." (Crosby, 2007, p. 12).

4.2 Data and research method

4.2.1 Dataset

This paper examines a further and not yet investigated potential source of return smoothing, namely the effect of timing of property appraisals on monthly fund returns, resulting in a reduction of observed fund investment risk. As German funds are obliged by the Investment Act (2008) to publish market values of individual properties, we use an internationally unique dataset of 4,296 property values derived by external independent appraisal experts within the years 2004 to 2007. Funds are obliged to have all properties appraised by an external expert *at least* once a year[43]. By re-valuing single properties sooner than twelve months however, they can influence which properties are being appraised within the same month. By valuing two properties with divergent value changes within the same calendar month, the annualized monthly[44] fund return would show less volatility than in the case of valuing the properties in subsequent months. Such a procedure would be feasible at least to some extent without prior knowledge of the appraisal result, for example in the case of one property being located in a rising market and the other one in a falling market, as most of the funds have a European investment focus.

42 For example, Levy and Schuck (2005) find evidence for New Zealand that clients exert influence on valuers by ways of expert and information power. Wolverton and Gallimore (1999) find for US appraisers that client feedback can have an influence on appraisals.

43 Due to cost reasons, funds usually do not have their properties appraised several times a year.

44 The majority of studies on fund returns of German open-end real estate funds use monthly data that is published by the Bundesverband Investment und Asset Management e. V. (BVI). To our knowledge, no study employs weekly or daily return data.

Results present strong evidence of the existence of valuation timing with the consequence of understating fund return volatility and thus investment risk. The missing link of property value changes and monthly fund returns questions the appropriateness of the funds' calculation and reporting of asset values.

The data on participation prices of the funds is taken from the Bundesverband Investment und Asset Management e.V. (BVI), which is an association that represents the interests of the German investment fund industry. The BVI publishes on a monthly basis participation prices, dividend distributions and capital flows of all German open-end real estate retail funds. Only those 24 funds have been chosen that are open to retail investors with no minimal participation amount[45]. Based on the monthly changes in participation prices and taking into account dividend payments, the monthly return of each fund has been calculated. This part of the dataset is easily available and has been analyzed in various studies before (Benk et al., 2008; Maurer et al., 2004; Thomas et al., 2009).

The novelty of this paper lies in the second part of the dataset. We analyzed the funds' annual statements of accounts and extracted all individual property market values for the years 2004 to 2007. Unfortunately, not all funds began to publish individual property market values as early as 2004. Only seven funds began to include individual property data into their reports as early as 2004. One year later, already 15 funds did so. From the year 2006 on, every fund publishes the necessary data. Table 4.1 gives an overview of the properties within the dataset. In total, 4,296 market values of individual properties from 2004 to 2007 are available for analysis. For the individual analysis years 2005 to 2007, this equals more than 1,000 properties with a market value between 60.9 bn EUR (2005) and 76.6 bn EUR (2006) each year.

4.2.2 Research hypotheses

The central idea of the paper is to contribute to the explanation of the stable return development of German open-end real estate retail funds. As GOEFs are invested in properties and to a minor extent in liquidity, return variance is likely to stem primarily from property returns. Property returns can be separated into stable net cash flows from leases and the more volatile return component of changes in properties' capital values. If properties were appraised on a daily basis, property value changes would influence fund returns continuously and in accordance with developments on the respective property markets. As property markets are not perfectly correlated and funds use this argument for investing globally, even a fund with a low number of properties in markets that correlate weakly or even negatively could result in less volatile fund returns than a fund with a high number of properties in positively correlated markets.

---

45 There exist funds with minimum participation amounts of e.g. 500,000 EUR. Those funds have been excluded, as they can rather be characterised as semi-institutional investment funds with different product characteristics.

Table 4.1 Properties of analyzed fund reports

Fund	2004		2005		2006		2007	
	# Proper-ties	Market value (EUR)	# Proper-ties	Market value (EUR)	# Proper-ties	Market value (EUR)	# Proper-ties	Market value (EUR)
AXA IMMOSELECT			29	1,344,508,000	40	1,934,196,000	58	2,708,144,000
CS EUROREAL (A) EUR					99	5,140,704,867	89	5,296,202,782
DEGI EUROPA					67	5,116,388,560	24	2,182,032,850
DEGI INTERNATIONAL			15	1,011,137,230	23	1,464,572,000	31	1,853,560,410
Deka-ImmobilienEuropa	100	7,183,800,165	99	7,296,700,485	84	6,161,357,348	77	5,787,234,130
Deka-ImmobilienGlobal	25	1,625,736,720	26	1,694,870,894	20	1,174,588,637	19	1,163,353,388
Deka-ImmobilienFonds	147	6,462,058,012	150	6,428,830,383	140	4,541,137,356	122	3,455,110,000
EURO ImmoProfil					78	1,777,637,000	78	1,718,623,000
grundbesitz-europa	133	6,962,703,000	128	6,567,471,000	94	4,299,460,000	28	2,333,399,000
grundbesitz-global	40	2,453,590,000	50	3,002,736,500	48	3,020,021,000	52	3,034,931,000
HANSAimmobilia					43	568,664,900	31	507,264,600
HAUS-INVEST europa			126	10,144,303,000	82	9,171,876,000	84	9,541,564,000
HAUS-INVEST global					13	1,336,011,000	16	1,132,020,000
INTER ImmoProfil					34	898,519,000	34	901,052,000
KanAm grundinvest Fonds			27	3,708,985,300	33	4,711,400,000		
MORGAN STANLEY P2 VALUE					22	858,675,589	40	2,112,546,443
SEB ImmoInvest			123	4,836,170,000	122	4,622,450,000	133	6,389,200,000
TMW Immobilien Weltfonds					10	411,344,918	13	668,790,000
UBS (D) Euroinvest Immobilien			58	2,587,300,000	60	2,644,400,000	53	2,947,100,000
UniImmo: Deutschland			90	6,354,040,000	73	5,245,661,000	39	3,592,180,000
UniImmo: Europa					82	5,247,085,000	67	5,174,101,000
UniImmo: Global			15	795,557,000	21	1,256,175,000	25	1,560,594,000
WestInvest 1	94	2,628,195,200	98	2,760,407,600	95	2,534,842,000	66	1,990,543,000
WestInvest InterSelect	37	2,186,996,000	40	2,392,607,000	40	2,421,044,000	44	2,750,895,000
Total	**576**	**29,503,079,097**	**1,074**	**60,925,624,392**	**1,423**	**76,558,211,175**	**1,223**	**68,800,440,603**

The table shows the number of properties and corresponding total market values in EUR of the 24 funds as year end 2004 to 2007. For KanAm grundinvest Fonds, data was not available to the time of the study, therefore only 23 funds are available for analysis in 2007.

However, as this paper wants to abstract from the question of the reliability of property valuation on the individual property level as well as on the aggregated level that results in the appraisal-based property indices describing market developments, correlation effects between property markets are not taken into consideration. This means that a high proportion of potential return variance resulting from divergent developments of regional property markets is neglected and the focus is put on the part that stems from property valuation on a yearly basis opposed to theoretical continuous valuations. If a single property represents a high proportion of a fund's assets and is appraised only once a year, the entire value change of the property over the whole year is reflected in the return of a single month. If property valuations are not arranged over the year with the aim to smooth potential return deviations, a high degree of asset concentration should result in an increased variance of monthly returns. Therefore, it is assumed that null hypothesis one cannot be rejected.

H1: "Asset concentration of portfolios and monthly return variance are positively correlated."

The second research hypothesis addresses the effect of extreme value changes of single properties on monthly fund returns. Many funds have single properties in their portfolios with capital values in excess of 10% of total net asset values[46]. Although we still do not know in which month the particular appraisal took place, we know that in *some* (single) month the strong value change must have influenced the return of the particular month. If monthly returns are not affected by strong value changes of single properties, this can be interpret as intended valuation timing to smooth strong return deviations. It is assumed that null hypothesis two cannot be rejected.

H2: "Strong absolute changes in market values of single properties are reflected in strong deviations of monthly fund returns"

4.3 Results

4.3.1 Distribution of fund returns

The distribution of fund returns shows a high density around the mean (i.e. being leptokurtic) which is in line with previous research on UK and US commingled real estate funds (Gallo et al., 2006; Young, 2008; Young et al., 2006). In the year 2005 few strongly negative returns result in a negative skewness of -1.17, while in 2006 and especially in 2007 only strongly positive returns deviate

46 As the property value changes directly affect the fund's equity position, independent from financial leverage, net asset value is the suitable point of reference.

from normality[47], resulting in a positive skewness of 1.60 and 5.41 (Table 4.2). The absence of strong negative fund returns is surprising, given the fact that in the respective years many fund properties decreased strongly in market value.

Table 4.2 Descriptive statistics of the monthly return distribution

	2005	2006	2007
Mean	0.25%	0.34%	0.46%
Standard deviation	0.27%	0.29%	0.47%
Skewness	-1.17	1.60	5.41
Kurtosis	10.21	4.42	42.24

The table shows statistics of monthly fund returns. The sample consists of 24 funds with each 12 monthly returns for 2007, resulting in 284 fund returns. As KanAm grundinvest Fonds, Morgan Stanley P2 Value and TMW Immobilien Weltfonds have been initiated after 2004-12-31, fewer returns enter the sample for 2005 and 2006. In total, 835 monthly fund returns are included from 2005-01-31 to 2007-12-31.

Previous studies have argued that serial correlation of property fund returns might be attributable to the appraisal process and refer to it as appraisal smoothing. Those smoothing effects can be found on the index level and on the disaggregate property level. For the individual property, smoothing would result from appraisers using either old transaction information or the previous appraisal of the same property as reference points (Clayton et al., 2001). With respect to the hypothesis regarding the correlation of asset concentration and fund return variance, the presence of serial correlation of fund returns at twelve month lag could be interpret as an effect of individual property value changes on fund returns. We therefore tested for serial correlation of monthly fund returns. Table 4.3 illustrates autocorrelation of fund returns for one to 13 months time lag where significantly high coefficients are indicated by bold figures. Out of the total of 24 funds, we analyzed serial correlation only for those twelve funds with at least 120 month return series available. We find significant correlation coefficients for six out of twelve funds, for three of them even in excess of 0.5. For the remaining six funds, correlation coefficients are not significant or even close to zero. For eleven or 13 months time lag however, no fund shows significant coefficients of autocorrelation. Therefore, it is not true for all funds that the yearly rhythm of property valuation results in serial correlation of fund returns with lag twelve.

4.3.2 Correlation of asset concentration and fund return variance

Asset concentration is measured via the Herfindahl-Hirschman Index (HHI). In its original context, the HHI measures industry concentration by comparing the size of individual firms to the size of the whole industry.

47 The Shapiro-Wilk test rejects normality at the 99% confidence level for all three years.

$$H := \frac{\sum_{i=1}^{N} a_i^2}{(\sum_{i=1}^{N} a_i)^2} = \sum_{i=1}^{N} (\frac{a_i}{N * \overline{a}})^2 \tag{4.1}$$

In the context of this paper, the index is used as an indicator for asset concentration within a property portfolio, where N is the number of funds' properties and a_i is the capital value of each property. By squaring property values individually before summation in the nominator while squaring the sum of all properties together in the denominator, the index approaches zero for funds with many identically small properties, while a single or dominant property within a fund results in an HHI value close to 1.

Table 4.4 shows the number of fund properties, the asset concentration index HHI, the highest value of a single fund property and the net asset values of funds in the years 2005, 2006 and 2007.

Unfortunately, the HHI can only be calculated for those funds which published valuation information on the single property level in the respective year. As expected, the funds with the highest number of properties tend to have the lowest HHI values. All funds with an HHI value of 0.02 or less have at least 76 properties in their portfolios. Nevertheless, the HHI seems to be the superior concentration measure in comparison to the mere number of properties, as the examples of the four funds Deka-ImmobilienEuropa, grundbesitz-global, EURO ImmoProfil and WestInvest 1 in 2007 show. All four funds have HHI values of 0.03, indicating that funds' properties are evenly distributed. However, grundbesitz-global achieves this index value with only 42 properties, while EURO ImmoProfil has 77 properties in the portfolio. The highest value of an individual property corresponds with the observation: While grundbesitz-global has 3.8% of NAV bound to one single property, EURO ImmoProfil has 11.2% of NAV invested in the property with the highest market value. This discrepancy of the two funds results in a good ranking position of rank four and rank five for the HHI, but in a bad ranking (17 of 22) position for EURO ImmoProfil in relation to asset concentration in one single property.

Figure 4.1 plots the asset concentration of funds (HHI, y-axis) against the corresponding standard deviations of monthly fund returns within the respective year (sd, x-axis) for the years 2005 to 2007. Due to mentioned data limitations in 2005 and 2006, only funds for which the HHI could be calculated enter the graph.

The assumed positive correlation between the asset concentration index and monthly return variance does not hold, as the correlation coefficient is not statistically significant. If any pattern can be derived, than the fact that nine out of 23 funds have a similar HHI value between 0.02 and 0.04 while the corresponding monthly return standard deviations vary widely between 0.1% and 0.5%.

Table 4.3 Autocorrelation of monthly fund returns 1998-2007

Lag	CS EUROREAL (A) EUR	Deka-ImmobilienEuropa	Deka-ImmobilienFonds	EURO ImmoProfil	grundbesitz-europa	DEGI EUROPA	HANSAimmobilia	HAUS-INVEST europa	SEB ImmoInvest	UniImmo: Deutschland	UniImmo: Europa	WestInvest 1	unweighted index
1	-0.10	**0.25**	**0.31**	0.17	**0.27**	0.17	0.19	0.12	0.05	**0.28**	**0.22**	0.11	**0.48**
2	-0.11	0.07	**0.27**	**0.38**	0.19	0.16	0.14	0.07	-0.09	**0.21**	0.07	0.16	**0.36**
3	0.03	0.14	0.18	**0.26**	**0.25**	0.09	-0.07	**0.33**	0.04	**0.24**	0.02	0.09	**0.45**
4	0.05	0.10	**0.27**	**0.32**	**0.24**	0.10	0.17	0.13	-0.11	**0.28**	0.06	**0.21**	**0.45**
5	0.02	0.11	**0.23**	0.19	0.11	0.08	0.19	0.12	-0.09	0.17	0.06	**0.26**	**0.38**
6	**0.47**	-0.02	0.16	**0.31**	0.06	-0.10	0.13	0.17	0.11	**0.24**	0.11	0.07	**0.29**
7	0.03	0.14	0.16	0.18	-0.02	-0.02	-0.04	0.16	-0.07	0.08	0.19	0.16	**0.34**
8	-0.08	0.08	0.14	**0.40**	0.07	0.01	-0.05	0.11	-0.02	0.20	0.03	0.13	**0.33**
9	0.19	-0.08	-0.10	0.04	0.04	0.07	0.03	**0.24**	-0.05	**0.22**	0.13	0.11	**0.32**
10	-0.12	0.08	0.10	**0.35**	-0.02	0.08	**0.24**	0.03	-0.02	**0.26**	0.17	**0.21**	**0.29**
11	-0.12	-0.02	0.05	0.14	0.09	**0.20**	0.14	-0.05	0.08	0.19	0.15	0.10	**0.24**
12	**0.59**	-0.01	0.02	**0.46**	0.03	0.14	0.17	**0.55**	**0.62**	**0.20**	0.19	**0.27**	**0.32**
13	0.05	-0.08	0.08	0.11	-0.08	0.12	0.04	0.15	0.01	0.12	0.05	0.09	**0.21**

The table shows autocorrelation of fund returns for one to 13 months time lag where significantly high coefficients of autocorrelation are indicated by bold figures. For each fund, the analysis is based on 120 monthly returns between 1997-12-31 and 2007-12-31. At lag twelve, only six out of twelve funds show significant (0.05 level) coefficients of serial correlation. On the index level (not capital weighted), serial correlation is significant at every time lag.

Table 4.4 Concentration of property portfolios 2005 to 2007 by funds

Fund	# Prop.	HHI	Rk	Max. single MV	NAV	Single prop. % NAV	Rk
Portfolio concentration 2005				(mill. EUR)			
Deka-Immo.Europa	91	0.021	1	346	8,884	3.9%	1
Deka-Immo.Fonds	139	0.021	2	371	4,921	7.5%	5
grundbesitz-europa	120	0.022	3	409	6,181	6.6%	4
WestInvest 1	86	0.026	4	139	2,999	4.6%	2
grundbesitz-global	36	0.035	5	134	2,290	5.9%	3
WestInvest InterS.	33	0.05	6	195	2,563	7.6%	6
Deka-Immo.Global	22	0.063	7	177	2,048	8.6%	7
Total	527	0.004		409	77,819	0.5%	
Portfolio concentration 2006							
SEB ImmoInvest	109	0.02	1	178	6,360	2.8%	1
Deka-Immo.Fonds	138	0.02	2	317	3,652	8.7%	7
HAUS-INVEST europa	75	0.02	3	429	8,538	5.0%	3
Deka-Immo.Europa	78	0.03	4	347	6,864	5.0%	4
WestInvest 1	83	0.03	5	135	2,213	6.1%	5
grundbesitz-europa	85	0.03	6	348	2,826	12.3%	12
grundbesitz-global	41	0.03	7	140	3,372	4.2%	2
WestInvest Inter.	36	0.05	8	212	2,564	8.2%	6
UniImmo: D.	67	0.05	9	535	5,020	10.7%	9
UBS Euro. Immo.	44	0.05	10	292	2,011	14.5%	14
AXA IMMOSELECT	29	0.08	11	276	2,519	10.9%	10
Deka-Immo.Global	17	0.09	12	184	1,747	10.6%	8
UniImmo: Global	12	0.12	13	154	1,369	11.3%	11
DEGI INT.	13	0.14	14	226	1,746	12.9%	13
Total	776	0.003		535	72,838	0.7%	
Portfolio concentration 2007							
SEB ImmoInvest	93	0.02	1	187	7,006	2.7%	1
Deka-Immo.Fonds	120	0.02	2	287	2,634	10.9%	16
CS EUROREAL	76	0.02	3	248	7,333	3.4%	3
HAUS-INVEST europa	70	0.03	4	400	10,081	4.0%	5
EURO ImmoProfil	77	0.03	5	165	1,470	11.2%	18
grundbesitz-global	42	0.03	6	135	3,588	3.8%	4
Deka-Immo.Europa	69	0.03	7	359	6,787	5.3%	7
WestInvest 1	63	0.03	8	145	1,927	7.5%	10
AXA IMMOSELECT	38	0.04	9	127	3,817	3.3%	2
UniImmo: Europa	54	0.04	10	400	5,448	7.3%	9
WestInvest InterS.	38	0.05	11	243	2,795	8.7%	12
UBS Euro. Immo.	42	0.05	12	319	2,290	13.9%	21
HANSAimmobilia	30	0.06	13	58	469	12.3%	19
INTER ImmoProfil	32	0.06	14	100	773	13.0%	20
UniImmo: D.	34	0.06	15	487	5,175	9.4%	13
DEGI EUROPA	21	0.08	16	212	4,527	4.7%	6
UniImmo: Global	18	0.08	17	175	1,837	9.5%	14
Deka-Immo.Global	15	0.09	18	187	1,689	11.0%	17
grundbesitz-europa	23	0.10	19	343	2,319	14.8%	22
M.S. P2 VALUE	21	0.10	20	136	1,911	7.1%	8
DEGI INT.	16	0.11	21	237	2,223	10.7%	15
HAUS-INVEST global	10	0.14	22	137	1,760	7.8%	11
TMW Immo. Weltf.	8	0.14	23	83	526	15.8%	23
Total	940	0.003		487	78,384	0.6%	

For the sub periods 2005, 2006 and 2007, the results are similar. Judging solely from monthly fund return variance, empirical findings give no indication that a fund with only 20 properties bears more idiosyncratic risk than a fund with more than 100 properties.

Hypothesis one regarding the correlation of asset concentration and monthly fund return variance **can be rejected**.

Figure 4.1 Asset concentration vs. standard deviation of monthly returns 2005-2007

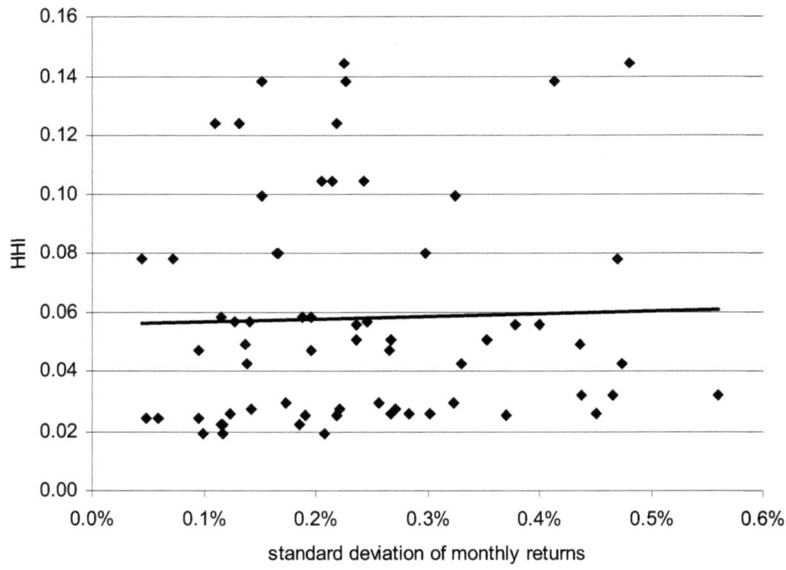

The figure plots the Herfindahl-Hirschman-Index of each portfolio of 2005, 2006 and 2007 against the respective standard deviation of monthly fund returns. The correlation of asset concentration and fund return volatility is not statistically significant at the 0.1 level.

4.3.3 Strong property value changes and return deflections

We test whether extreme value changes of single properties influence return deviations (hypothesis 2). Because funds publish information on appraisal values of their properties only once a year, it is not possible to directly link value changes of properties to changes in monthly participation prices and derived fund returns. Figure 4.2 illustrates the problem of the data mismatch.

Figure 4.2 Property value changes and monthly returns of UniImmo: Europa in 2007

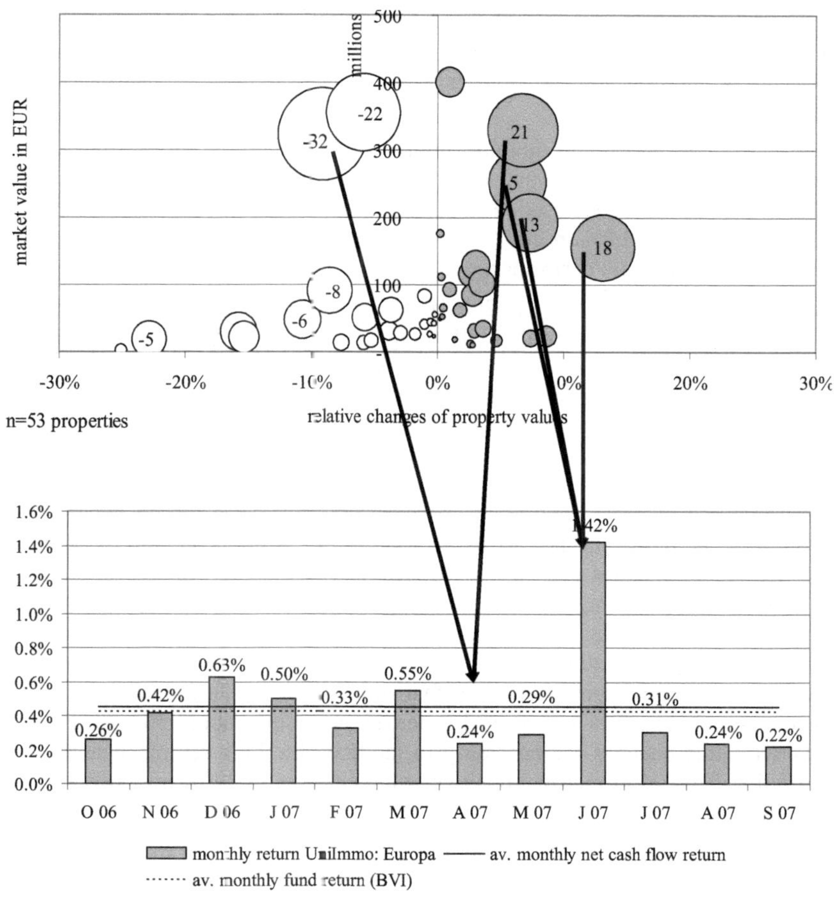

The upper part of the illustration summarizes the relevant information on value changes of 53 standing investment[48] fund properties of UniImmo: Europa in report year 2007. The x-position of the bubbles stands for the relative change in

48 Property sales, partial sales or developments have not been taken into consideration as their value changes do not stem solely from the valuation process. As funds to not publish information on capital improvements on the individual property level, this figure cannot be included in the calculation of property value changes. We regard this issue as of minor importance, because developments (with high capital improvements by definition) are excluded anyways. The calculated change of market values is however in line with the suggestion of Young (2005, p. 212) to adjust the NPI Capital Return calculation.

value (DMV) that every property realized from 2006-10-01 to 2007-09-30, as September is the month UniImmo: Europa reports to. The y-position depicts the value of every property in EUR as to 2007-09-30. The size of the bubble area stands for the absolute value change in EUR of every property within the report year. Grey bubbles indicate value gains while white bubbles indicate decreases in value.

The lower part shows the monthly returns of UniImmo: Europa from October 2006 to September 2007, the same time span in which the property value changes (upper part) occurred. The solid line indicates the fund's net cash flow return, reported at 5.2% in 2007, distributed evenly over twelve months to give an indication[49] of fund performance in the absence of property value changes.

As the fund's net asset value in 2007 is 5.4 bn EUR, a negative value change of a single property of -32 mill. EUR (biggest white bubble) should result - all other things equal - in a decrease of the monthly fund return[50] by about -0.6%, turning nominal fund performance negative. However, we see no single negative return in 2007, not even a return below 0.2%. The most probable assumption is that in the month with the most negative value change of a single property one or more properties with positive value changes were appraised as well. The arrows indicate *possible* bundles of appraised properties that could result in the observed fund return. In the case of the -32 mill. EUR appraisal, at least appraisals with value changes of +20 mill. EUR are necessary to prevent the monthly fund return from falling below 0.2%. However, we still do not know whether this was the case in August 2007, as indicated, or in any other month. In case of the extreme positive return of June 2007 we still do not know which of the positive value changes were realised in that month, but as the monthly return exceeds the net cash flow return by 1.0 percentage points, about 50 mill. EUR of positive value changes are necessary to facilitate the high return, meaning that more than 50% of properties' positive value changes in 2007 are likely to have occurred in June.

In accordance with the argumentation presented above, the problem of data mismatch is encountered by focusing on those funds' properties with the highest absolute value changes in the respective years. The idea is that if property valuations are not planned to level out positive and negative value changes but are randomly distributed over the year, strong value changes of single properties should at least in some cases be reflected in one monthly return of the respective year. Therefore, Table 4.5 shows the maximum value changes of single properties of each fund in the years 2005 to 2007 as percentage of net asset value. A change in NAV is directly reflected in fund returns. For example, if the net cash

49 The indication is not very accurate, as important parameters of fund return like the return on liquid assets are not taken into consideration.

50 The value changes directly affect the fund's equity position, regardless of the employed financial leverage.

flow return of a fund together with liquidity returns less costs result in a monthly return of 0.3% and, all other things being equal, a fund's property is appraised in this month with a negative value change of 1% of NAV, the fund's return turns from plus 0.3% into minus 0.7%. The standard deviations of monthly fund returns vary among funds, but on average the standard deviation over all funds and the three years is 0.3% per month. Therefore, the single effect of the appraisal of the properties with the most extreme value changes, all other thing being equal, would result in case of the bold figures in a fund return varying by more than 0.9% or three standard deviations from the mean of the arguably smoothed return series.

Table 4.5 Maximum value changes of single properties as percentage of NAV

Fund	Highest positive value change of single property as % NAV			Highest negative value change of single property as % NAV		
	2005	2006	2007	2005	2006	2007
AXA IMMOSELECT		0.5%	0.3%		-0.2%	-0.1%
CS EUROREAL			0.4%			-0.1%
DEGI EUROPA			**0.8%**			-0.4%
DEGI INT.		0.4%	**1.5%**			-0.5%
Deka-ImmobilienEuropa	0.1%	0.4%	0.5%	-0.2%	-0.2%	-0.1%
Deka-ImmobilienGlobal	**0.7%**	**0.8%**	0.4%	-0.5%	-0.3%	-0.3%
Deka-ImmoFonds	**0.8%**	**2.2%**	0.4%	-0.3%	**-1.4%**	**-1.2%**
EURO ImmoProfil			0.2%			**-1.9%**
grundbesitz-europa	0.2%	**0.9%**	0.3%	-0.5%	**-1.4%**	-0.3%
grundbesitz-global	**0.6%**	0.2%	0.3%	**-0.6%**	-0.3%	-0.4%
HANSAimmobilia			0.5%			**-0.7%**
HAUS-INVEST europa		**0.8%**	**1.4%**		-0.3%	**-0.6%**
HAUS-INVEST global			**0.9%**			**-0.7%**
INTER ImmoProfil			**0.6%**			-0.6%
KanAm grundinv. Fonds		**1.9%**			-0.4%	
M.S. P2 VALUE			0.3%			0.0%
SEB ImmoInvest		0.1%	0.5%		-0.3%	-0.3%
TMW Immobilien Weltf.			0.3%			**-0.7%**
UBS (D) Euro. Immo.		**1.0%**	**1.2%**		**-0.7%**	-0.1%
UniImmo: Deutschland		0.4%	0.6%		-0.3%	-0.6%
UniImmo: Europa			0.4%			-0.6%
UniImmo: Global		0.4%	0.5%		**-0.8%**	**-1.7%**
WestInvest 1	0.1%		**0.7%**	-0.1%	-0.2%	-0.5%
WestInvest InterS.	0.2%	**0.7%**	**1.1%**	-0.3%	-0.1%	-0.2%

Figure 4.3 illustrates the idea of matching assumed value changes in monthly fund returns and high value changes of single properties for the year 2007. The dotted lines indicate the highest and the lowest monthly fund returns in the re-

spective twelve month interval[51] the property valuations took place. The crosses stand for the most extreme positive and negative value changes as percentage of NAV of a single property. For example, in case of DEGI INTERNATIONAL it is surprising that the value change of a single property would have resulted in a positive fund return of 1.6%, neglecting the net cash flow return, but the highest monthly return over the entire year was only 1.0%, even inclusive the net cash flow return. Again, in the single case, this might be due to chance, and in the same month a strong negative property value change could have affected the fund return as well, levelling out the effect. However, every single fund portfolio experienced property devaluations that, as a single event without being also accompanied by other positive value changes, would have resulted in monthly fund returns far more negative than the most negative return in the whole year. Results for the years 2005 and 2006 are similar. **Hypothesis two can be rejected,** as strong value changes of single properties do not cause strong fund return deflections.

Figure 4.3 Range of monthly returns vs. value changes of single properties 2007

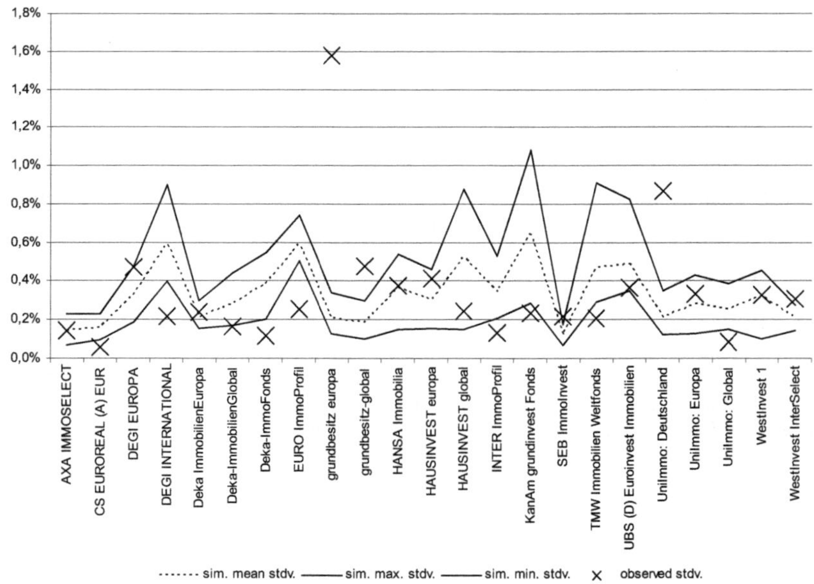

The figure shows the bandwidth of monthly fund returns as given by the most positive and the most negative returns of analysis year 2007. The crosses illustrate the effect on a fund return that would result - all other things equal - from the realization of the most positive (+) and the most negative (x) value change.

---

51 Those intervals differ by funds, as many funds report to end September, many to end December and few to other months.

4.3.4 Simulation of randomly distributed appraisals

The less than expected effect of single property valuations on monthly fund returns supports the assumption that property valuations affect fund returns not randomly but are rather planned to level out strong return deviations. In a Monte Carlo Simulation[52], the observed value changes of funds' properties in 2007 are randomly distributed over the twelve months of the corresponding reporting periods. In the case of UniImmo: Europa (Figure 4.2) for example, the 53 value changes in 2007 are distributed randomly over twelve months. For each portfolio, the procedure is repeated 1,000 times, creating 1,000 different sets of potential timing structures of valuations. For each set, minimum, maximum and mean standard deviations of the resulting value changes are calculated. Figure 4.3 illustrates the results graphically. The crosses indicate actual (observed) monthly return variance, while the lines show the monthly return variance that would have stemmed solely from property valuations.

In case of funds like grundbesitz-europa or UniImmo: Deutschland the observed return variance is even higher than the maximum return variance of 1,000 iterations of randomly distributed property valuations. This result is not surprising, as the effect of valuation timing is only one source of fund return variance. Gains from selling off properties are likely to have influenced return volatility of the funds afore mentioned strongly. Surprising however is the case of eight out of 23 funds, where the observed return variance falls below the minimal return variance in 1,000 iterations of the variance solely stemming from property valuations.

The fact that a random distribution of value changes in 2007 over the twelve months results in many cases in a much higher return variance than the observed total return variance can be interpret as an indication for return variance smoothing through valuation timing. One has to bear in mind that the simulated return variance addresses only that part of return variance that comes from yearly valuations as contrasted to continuous valuations. Variance arising from divergent developments on different property markets, property developments or (portfolio) sales is not even considered and would in many cases even increase fund return variance in addition to the simulated source of return variance.

---

52 The term "Monte Carlo method' was coined by physicists working on nuclear weapon projects in the Los Alamos National Laboratory (Metropolis, 1987). The term stands for a class of algorithms that rely on repeated sampling to calculate results. Within the field of real estate, the method has been applied as well, but not within the presented context (Baroni, Barthélémy, & Mokrane, 2007; Farncombe & Waller, 2007; Fingleton, 2008; Hoesli, Jani, & Bender, 2006; Wofford, 1978). An important difference to the bootstrap approach is that the bootstrap relies on real observations, while the Monte Carlo method can use hypothetical data (Manly, 2007), which is the case when we distribute appraisals randomly over calendar months.

Figure 4.4 Simulation: Return variance with randomly distributed appraisals in 2007

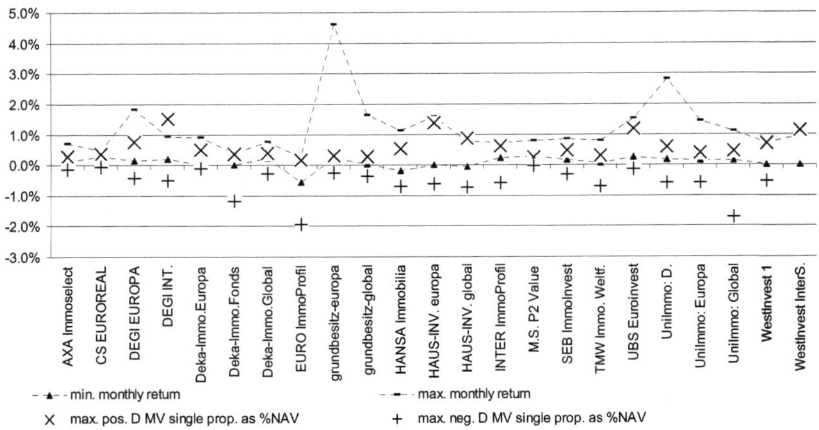

In a final step the regression analysis to test hypothesis one on the correlation of asset concentration and fund return variance is repeated for the simulated fund return variance. Figure 4.5 plots the funds' HHI values against the mean of simulated return variance stemming from the randomly distributions of property value changes. Adjusted R squared reaches 14.7% and even 16.5% for the sub period 2007. In both linear models, hypothesis one of a positive correlation between asset concentration and (simulated) return variance cannot be rejected at the 0.05 confidence level (p-values of 0.035 and 0.015).

It can be concluded that if property valuations of funds' properties occurred randomly over the year, a positive correlation of funds' asset concentration and monthly return variance would result. As this holds not true for observed monthly returns, a further indication for valuation timing with the result of smoothed return volatility is presented.

4.4 *Conclusion*

The results present a strong indication for substantial timing effects of property valuations on the variance of monthly fund returns. For most funds, it can be shown that high value changes of single properties did not result in extreme return deflections in the respective (although unknown) months. Monthly fund returns exhibit the following characteristics that indicate intended valuation timing and that have to be considered when analyzing fund returns in portfolio optimisation procedures of open-end real estate retail fund data:

Figure 4.5 Asset concentration vs. simulated volatility of monthly returns 2005-2007

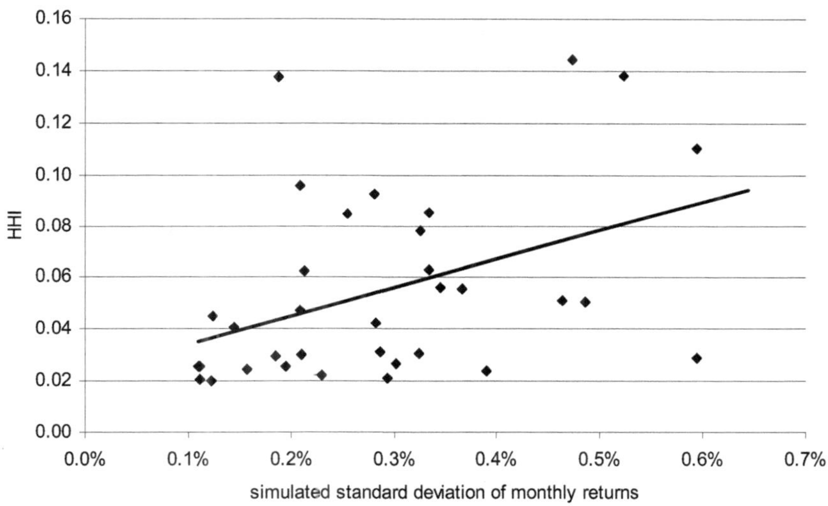

- The fund return distribution is skewed and highly leptokurtic, with positive and negative fat tails
- Only half of the funds exhibit autocorrelation of lag twelve in monthly fund returns
- Asset concentration has no influence on observed fund return variance
- Strong value changes of single properties do not result in strong return deflections

The existence of valuation timing by the fund management with the effect of smoothing monthly fund returns is problematic for several reasons. As most performance benchmarks are based on a mean/ variance framework, return smoothing decreases fund return variance and thus improves the ranking position of the respective fund. In multi asset portfolio optimisation applications, smoothed returns can result in an over allocation of the respective asset to the disadvantage of the investor. Regarding theory-based research like the study of Bannier et al. (2008), we argue that our empirical findings should be integrated. Their proposal[53] of increasing the property valuation frequency to better match participation prices and fund asset values cannot convince in the presence of valuation timing and the missing link of property value changes and monthly participation prices.

From the missing link of property performance and monthly fund returns arises the question which factors actually have an influence on monthly fund returns? Judging from significant serial correlation of *some* fund returns at the twelve months lag, we will continue to examine calendar anomalies to explain monthly fund returns of German open-end real estate retail funds.

---

53 The proposal to increase valuation frequency has also been part of an initiative of BVI to improve fund stability in the aftermath of the fund crisis in 2005.

5 Calendar anomalies in German open-end fund returns

5.1 Introduction

It has been shown that returns of GOEFs are smoothed due to the timing of property valuations (chapter 4). With respect to their German properties, there is evidence that the majority of funds did influence property appraisals in such a way that the strong yield compression in 2006 and 2007 was not reflected in value gains (chapter 2). As a big proportion of those German properties was sold in 2006 and 2007 close to the market values which had not been appreciated in the years before, it is clear that market values in 2006 and 2007 were a quiet close estimate of asset prices at this point of time. One explanation for that is that properties may have been overvalued before 2006. But whether one agrees on the overvaluation argument or not, the fact that German properties did not gain significantly in market value in 2006 and 2007 can be seen as smoothing of property value changes in times of rising markets. Chapter 3 shows that foreign properties of GOEFs do not reflect changes in cap rates to the same extent as properties held by local market participants do. Especially in the case of the UK market it is evident that valuations of GOEFs' properties are smoothed, if we assume that local valuations truly reflect market movements. All three presented essays find smoothing effects within GOEFs, either on the portfolio level (chapter 4) or on the individual property level (chapters 2 and 3). Therefore, we present a **review of smoothing effects** in international real estate research. We deepen into the issue of autocorrelation of fund returns and present evidence that at least a big proportion of observed serial correlation of GOEFs returns does not stem from the valuation process on the property level, but is rather due to **calendar anomalies** of fund returns.

5.2 Appraisal smoothing within German open-end real estate funds

In one of the most influential studies on direct real estate performance measurement, Geltner (1989a) presents a theory of smoothing of real estate appraisals and suggests a methodology to unsmooth property returns on the index level to reveal "real" asset volatility. He argues that two levels of smoothing can enter property index returns: Firstly, at the disaggregate level of individual property appraisals over time and secondly at the aggregate index level. He refers to the first level of smoothing as "lack of confidence" and argues that the appraiser cannot be certain if his current estimate of market value meets exactly the true market value. He argues that given market value estimates of the same property for the previous year (as it is usually the case for commingled real estate funds), appraisers will consider the previous years estimate to at least some extent. Geltner introduces a "confidence factor" α with $0 <= \alpha <= 1$ and suggests a modelling of the appraised property value V^* at time t as:

$$V_t^* = \alpha V_t + (1-\alpha)V_{t-1}^* \tag{5.1}$$

The incorporation of previous appraisals into the actual appraisal results in an exponentially weighted moving average of true returns.

The second level of smoothing he refers to as the "valuation timing" issue. He argues that appraisers will base the valuation at least to some extent on actual transaction prices of properties sold in the respective area. Because those sales of similar properties will have occurred over a past period of time, the resulting appraisal value again will be a moving average of past true values, and the appraised portfolio value will also be a moving average of past appraised values. He argues that a moving average of a stochastic process is a "smoothed" version of the underlying stochastic process that shows less variation than the original process. This is why both presented factors introduce smoothing into the time series of appraised returns. He concludes that strong autocorrelation in return series is a sign for smoothed returns, finds US direct property returns to be highly autocorrelated and presents a methodology to unsmooth the return series.

Since then, the issue of unveiling unbiased real estate returns[54] has gained major attention within real estate research (Domrow & Turnbull, 2004). The majority of studies start from the ascertainment that property (fund) returns are autocorrelated and show low volatility. The resulting superiority of real estate returns indicated by customary performance measures like the Sharpe Ratio has frequently been questioned (e.g Bond & Hwang, 2003). With the exception of Lai and Wang (1998), research reasons that the observed return series underestimate the "true" return volatility which cannot be observed as real estate transactions occur infrequently. Following Geltner's argument and partly extending his assumptions regarding to which factors lead to valuation anchoring, many studies "unsmooth" real estate returns using the autoregressive return component. The resulting "unsmoothed" indices do not show serial correlation anymore by definition, and are much more volatile than the original time series. Table 5.1 updates a summary of Geltner, MacGregor, and Schwann (2003) on smoothing factors applied in various studies. The right column states the factors that were applied to the standard deviations of the original return series. As all studies started with return series that are serially correlation, the "unsmoothed" returns are much more volatile than the original ones. Results range from plus 57% (Barkham & Geltner, 1994) to plus 602% (Maurer et al., 2004) increase of return volatility as compared to the original time series.

Maurer et al. (2004) and Maurer and Sebastian (2002) also concede that returns of GOEFs may be smoothed, but they argue in line with Hoesli and Hamelink (1996) that the smoothed returns are those that were actually received by the investors.

---

54 Besides real estate, research on smoothing and lagging patterns exist in other illiquid asset classes such as hedge fund investment as well (e.g. Getmansky, Lo, & Makarov, 2004).

Table 5.1 Desmoothing factors applied to appraisal-based indices

Study	Country	Factor applied to standard deviation
Ross and Zisler (1991)	US	3-5
Brown (1991)	UK	3.44
MacGregor and Nanthakumaran (1992)	UK	2.86
Geltner (1993)	US	2
Fisher, Geltner, and Webb (1994)	US	1.58-1.66
Barkham and Geltner (1994)	UK	1.57
Newell and MacFarlane (1996)	UK	3.45
Maurer et al. (2004)	GER	2.79-6.02
Wang (2006)	UK	1.5-1.9
Benk et al. (2008)[55]	GER	1.6

Source: Geltner, MacGregor, and Schwann (2003), amended

We agree upon the theoretical appeal of the argument, only empirical evidence from our sample of German open-end real estate funds return series and the corresponding property appraisals is in contrast to it. Regarding the "lack of confidence" argument, we will show that at least for some portfolios appraisers did not use information from previous appraisals in current appraisals. Regarding the "valuation timing" argument, we will show that in most portfolios appraisers did not incorporate recent transactions into their appraisals. As fund returns of GOEFs nevertheless are highly autocorrelated, we will show that calendar anomalies are better suited to explain autocorrelation in fund returns.

Yiu et al. (2006) present a comprehensive literature review on appraisal smoothing. They summarize more than 40 studies and categorize the various research designs (Figure 5.1). They use a very broad valuation context of development land to discuss many potential biases. They start with the argument that the neglect of the intrinsic option value of the land can cause a systematic downward bias in valuations (Option Value Hypothesis). The same effect will occur when buyers see more development opportunities and more possibilities to lift efficiencies than the valuer does. The consequence is that the buyer will be ready to pay a higher price than the valuer would assume, and thus induce a systematic downward bias in valuations (Different Base-of-Valuation Hypothesis). With respect to the presented context of GOEF investments of developed and fully let (at least at the time of purchase) commercial properties, those potential systematic biases are of minor concern. The effect of purely random appraisal (Purely Random) bias is also not relevant in the given context as we consider only valuation effects of individual properties on the portfolio level on which random appraisal biases should cancel out. The mentioned possibility of random bias towards higher variance (Overreaction) does not fit to the smooth return structure. Basically, three kinds of bias remain to explain smoothed returns of GOEFs: Firstly, the effect of lagged aggregation of property market movements

55 The study of Benk et al. (2008) has not been published in a scientific journal. However, it is the only research that explicitly desmoothes returns of GOEFs.

on the index level (Valuation Timing), secondly anchoring biases (either to previous estimates, asking prices or other references) and thirdly client influence. The first two possibilities do not convince given the results of chapter 2 and chapter 3. In the case of Deka-ImmobilienFonds in 2006 where the entire German property portfolio was devalued by 18.8%[56] on average despite rising markets, anchoring to previous transaction data was certainly not the case. Neither were the values of the previous value estimates maintained, as this would not explain a strong devaluation. With respect to chapter 4, which shows that GOEFs did not change UK property values as quickly as the local market participants did, it may be the case that valuers anchored their appraisals to previous years' estimates. In this case however, such behaviour has to be considered as systematic bias[57], because appraisers were aware that local valuers did mark values down in an unprecedented extent. According to the previously discussed classification of Yiu et al. (2006), it can be concluded that smoothed returns of GOEFs most likely result from direct or indirect forms of client influence on the valuations of fund properties.

5.3 Data

We use monthly return data from 1993 through 2008 for all funds that were set up before 1993 and are still available for investment. The year 1993 seems a good trade off between the length of the time series of 16 years and the width of the sample as eleven funds are available. For analysis, 2,112 monthly returns are available. We decided to exclude two fund returns of grundbesitz-europa in 2007. They are considered to be outliers as they are in excess of 4% given a standard deviation of the fund's returns of 0.510% and z-values in excess of 8.9. They are a direct consequence of a portfolio sale of German properties in 2007. For a performance evaluation on fund level, this procedure would not be suitable of course, as those two months have massive consequences on the fund performance in 2007 and even on the ten-year-performance. As we are interested in recurrent return patterns rather than in the aggregate return over the entire period, the exclusion of those returns seems justifiable and therefore 2,110 fund returns of eleven funds are available for analysis. Over all funds and years, the mean of monthly returns is 0.369% with a standard deviation of 0.279%.

---

56 The statement of accounts for the report year 2006 of Deka-ImmobilienFonds reports the value change of the German property portfolio to be -18.8% (p. 23). However, the unprecedented devaluation of a substantial proportion of a GOEF property portfolio did not result in a negative fund return, as Deka Bank subsidized the fund return by 9.1% of fund NAV (p. 24) such that the fund return was 2.0% in 2006 and not -7.1% as it would have been the case without the subsidy.

57 We argue that German appraisers were biased because we assume that UK appraisers better reflected market developments in times of the beginning of the financial crises in 2007. Solely judging from significantly deviating appraisals, both sides could be biased equally.

Figure 5.1 Sources of appraisal bias

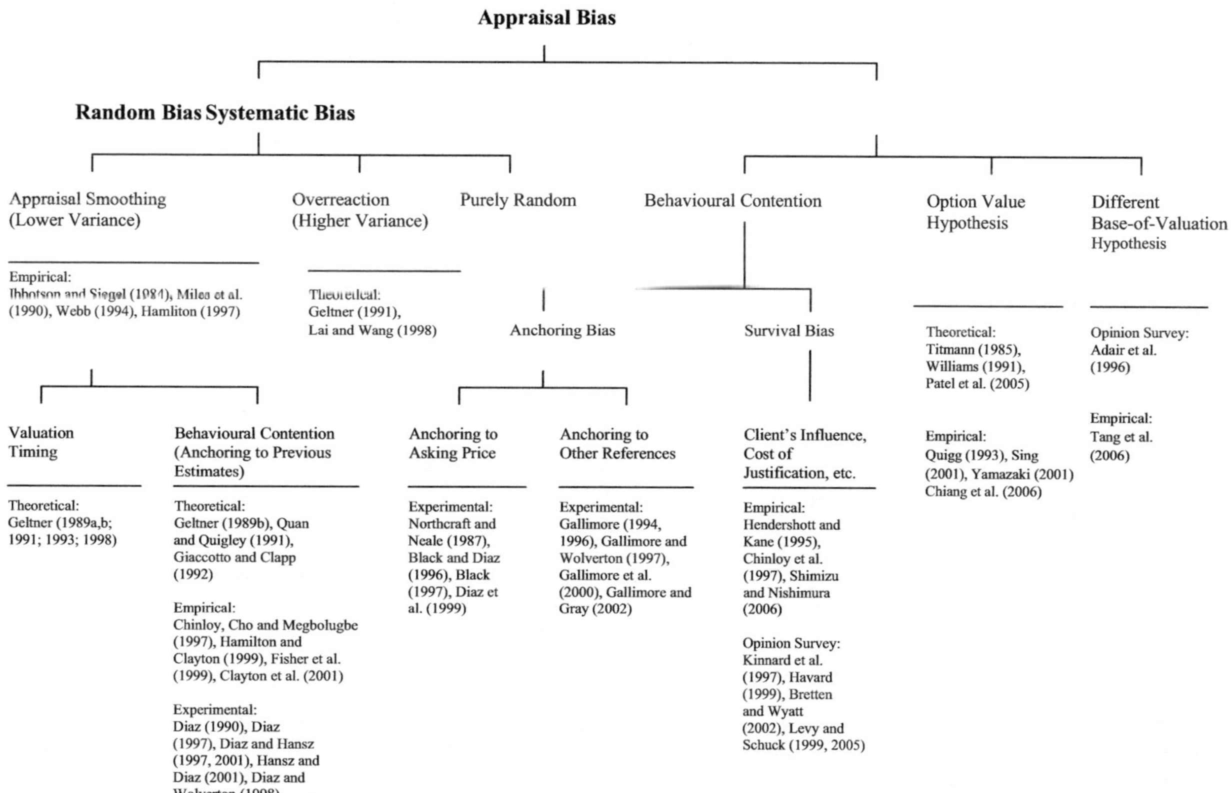

Source: Yiu et al. (2006)

On an annualised basis, a mean return of 4.52% can be considered very low, given that in the same period the money market represented by the EURIBOR yielded 3.75% and the bond market represented by the REXP achieved a 6.20% return. The annualised standard deviation of all fund returns is 0.96%, which is about twice the figure of the money market (0.38%) and less than one third of the bond market (3.25%). The distribution is slightly left skewed (skewness: -0.313) but highly leptokurtic with a kurtosis of 16.1. Figure 5.2 shows mean monthly fund returns and indicates the 95% confidence intervals of the means.

While the mean returns of most funds range evenly between 0.33% and 0.40%, returns of SEB ImmoInvest and EURO ImmoProfil differ significantly. The ranges of the confidence intervals reveal that standard errors of the funds are similar as well, although SEB ImmoInvest shows the narrowest interval, while EURO ImmoProfil has the widest interval.

5.4 Results

5.4.1 Empirical evidence of autocorrelation in fund returns

Table 5.2 illustrates autocorrelation of fund returns for time lags between one and 13 months where significant coefficients of autocorrelation at the 0.05 level are indicated by bold figures. Ten out of eleven funds show significantly positive serial correlation for one month time lag. For every time lag from two to 13 months, between four and seven funds have significant coefficients of correlation. The fact that funds held money market investments and cash between 1993 and 2008 on average of a minimum of 3.9% (HANSAimmobilia) to a maximum of 21.7% (CS EUROREAL)[58] of fund volume contributes to the explanation of lagged returns in the short term, as money market returns are highly autocorrelated themselves.For lag twelve, however, eight out of eleven funds exhibit significant serial correlation, and in the case of SEB ImmoInvest and HAUS-INVEST europa with very high coefficients of 0.541 and 0.397. The funds grundbesitz-europa and UniImmo: Europa are the exceptions to the rule, as they hardly exhibit any autocorrelation. The IPD open-end fund index OFIX-10 shows significant serial correlation for all time lags. Maurer et al. (2004) investigate autocorrelation of GOEF index returns from 1975 to 2003 and show similar results. They even report serial correlation at lag twelve to be 0.42 and assume that: "This may be evidence for annual events, e.g. appraisals of property, having an impact on the autocorrelation structure of returns" (p. 219).

---

58 The high ratio of money market investments and cash (unweighted average) of CS EUROEAL (A) EUR is due to the fact that the fund has been initiated in 1992, with high cash proportions in the first years.

Figure 5.2 Mean monthly fund returns 1993-2008 by fund

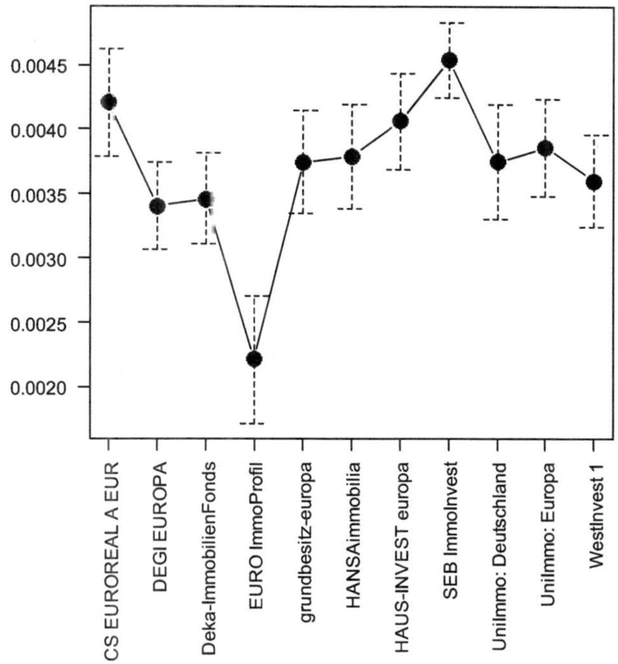

Their argument either relies on the assumption that the same properties are being appraised *exactly* at a twelve months interval or that in some months more properties are being appraised than in other months, with the consequence that a bigger proportion of yearly property value changes fall into those months. The first assumption is in contrast to findings of chapter 4, where evidence is presented that valuations are consciously timed and thus do not simply follow a twelve month interval. The second assumption is in contrast to the idea of a rolling valuation in which value changes on the portfolio level are to be tracked evenly through the year.

Judging solely from serial correlation on the index level, one could argue that the autocorrelation stems from the infrequent and smoothed appraisal process of fund properties. The fact that autocorrelation patterns differ significantly between funds however suggests that the causes for serial correlation of fund returns might differ by fund and are not solely attributable to the nature of the appraisal process.

5.4.2 Fund returns by calendar month

Table 5.3 shows mean monthly fund returns from 1993 to 2008 by calendar month. Bold type figures highlight the months with the highest average return over the 16 years, and grey shading of the cells indicates the month to which funds report to59. For four out of eleven funds, the highest average fund returns fall into December and two into September, which is the reporting month of the respective funds. Interestingly, the funds with the highest coefficients of autocorrelation at lag twelve, namely SEB ImmoInvest and HAUS-INVEST europa are also the two funds with the highest average returns in one single month. In case of HAUS-INVEST europa, an average monthly fund return of 0.69% in September equals an annualized return of 8%, which is about twice the figure of the average over all twelve calendar months. The positive September returns are preceded by below average returns of 0.33% in August and followed by weak returns of 0.31% in October. In case of SEB ImmoInvest, December returns of 0.60% are almost twice as high as exceptionally low September returns. Before we deepen into the issue of calendar anomalies of open-end funds, it can be concluded that at least part of the autocorrelation observed in fund returns can be attributed to fund returns that differ by calendar month.

Figure 5.3 shows mean fund returns over all eleven funds and 192 months. The solid line indicates the average monthly return over all calendar months. The funds realised on average a nominal return of 0.37% per month or 4.52% on an annual basis from 1993 through 2008. In September however, mean returns were 0.45% or 5.56% annualised, and in June only 0.31%, or 3.83% annualised.

To test whether returns differ significantly by calendar month, we refer to previous research on calendar anomalies. No research exists on month-of-the-year effects for real estate mutual funds. Studies on calendar anomalies within real estate mainly focus on REIT returns. The two main calendar anomalies investigated are the day-of-the-week effect[60] and the January-effect[61]. With respect to the January-effect, Friday and Peterson (1997), Redman et al. (1997), Friday and Higgins (2000), Lee, M-L. and Lee, M-T. (2003), and Hardin et al. (2005) report significantly higher returns in January due to tax-loss effects. Higher returns in September are not found in any of the mentioned studies.

---

59 HANSAimmobilia changed the reporting period from October to December in 2006.

60 See e.g. Abraham and Ikenberry (1994), Chan, Leung, and Wang (2005), Friday and Higgins (2000), Keim and Stambaugh (1984), MacFarland, Pettit, and Sung (1982), Wang, Li, and Erickson (1997).

61 For example Cho, Kawaguchi, and Shilling (2003) also find significant serial correlation of UK monthly property returns with lag twelve, but they do not further investigate whether the calendar month is part of the underlying reason.

Table 5.2 Autocorrelation of monthly fund returns 1993-2008

time lag in months	CS_EUROREAL	DEGI_EUROPA	Deka_ImmobilienFonds	EURO_ImmoProfil	grundbesitz_europa	HANSAimmobilia	HAUSINVEST_europa	SEB_ImmoInvest	UniImmo_Deutschland	UniImmo_Europa	WestInvest_1	OFIX_10	EURIBOR	REXP	# funds sig. coefficients
lag 1	**0.164**	**0.285**	**0.431**	**0.286**	**0.240**	**0.325**	**0.162**	**0.224**	**0.234**	**0.258**	0.078	**0.505**	**0.990**	**0.183**	10
lag 2	-0.064	**0.230**	**0.310**	**0.380**	**0.245**	**0.145**	0.077	0.001	**0.218**	0.130	**0.198**	**0.435**	**0.975**	0.052	6
lag 3	0.047	**0.239**	**0.241**	**0.364**	**0.167**	0.111	**0.283**	0.009	**0.356**	0.122	**0.158**	**0.397**	**0.961**	0.089	6
lag 4	-0.097	**0.238**	**0.313**	**0.471**	**0.210**	**0.207**	**0.171**	-0.026	**0.214**	0.132	**0.185**	**0.442**	**0.946**	0.025	7
lag 5	-0.019	**0.200**	**0.325**	**0.370**	0.094	**0.208**	**0.171**	0.066	**0.155**	0.140	0.135	**0.360**	**0.925**	-0.062	6
lag 6	0.071	0.125	**0.297**	**0.352**	0.075	**0.157**	**0.154**	**0.169**	**0.223**	0.102	**0.163**	**0.309**	**0.899**	-0.042	7
lag 7	**0.240**	0.111	**0.273**	**0.388**	0.015	0.077	**0.146**	-0.013	0.081	**0.186**	**0.192**	**0.300**	**0.869**	0.010	6
lag 8	**0.173**	**0.162**	**0.318**	**0.489**	0.074	0.049	0.123	-0.026	0.111	0.014	**0.194**	**0.340**	**0.840**	0.077	5
lag 9	0.039	0.105	0.124	**0.274**	0.061	0.062	**0.171**	0.008	**0.148**	0.042	0.100	**0.233**	**0.806**	-0.038	3
lag 10	-0.083	**0.245**	0.130	**0.344**	0.017	**0.176**	0.052	0.127	0.125	0.093	**0.170**	**0.222**	**0.770**	-0.014	4
lag 11	**-0.162**	**0.157**	0.076	**0.293**	0.061	**0.175**	0.008	**0.218**	0.069	0.073	0.039	**0.173**	**0.730**	-0.067	5
lag 12	0.016	**0.274**	0.089	**0.380**	0.088	**0.227**	**0.397**	**0.541**	**0.167**	**0.149**	**0.279**	**0.221**	**0.686**	-0.099	8
lag 13	-0.061	**0.257**	**0.192**	**0.383**	-0.009	0.074	0.097	**0.178**	0.077	0.100	0.057	**0.207**	**0.641**	-0.131	4

Table 5.3 Mean monthly fund returns 1993-2008 by calendar month and fund

Fund	January	February	March	April	May	June	July	August	September	October	November	December
CS EUROREAL (A) EUR	0.43%	0.30%	0.34%	0.48%	0.45%	0.47%	0.41%	0.34%	0.46%	0.32%	0.50%	**0.55%**
DEGI EUROPA	0.40%	0.31%	0.30%	0.33%	0.32%	0.25%	0.38%	0.26%	0.41%	0.35%	0.35%	**0.43%**
Deka-ImmobilienFonds	0.40%	0.35%	0.33%	0.36%	0.27%	0.29%	**0.42%**	0.35%	0.36%	0.33%	0.35%	0.35%
EURO ImmoProfil	0.30%	0.24%	0.26%	0.21%	0.24%	0.05%	0.29%	0.20%	0.29%	-0.02%	**0.33%**	0.24%
grundbesitz-europa	0.37%	0.36%	0.34%	0.34%	0.26%	0.28%	0.42%	0.38%	**0.57%**	0.36%	0.36%	0.46%
HANSAimmobilia	0.43%	0.41%	0.31%	0.46%	0.25%	0.21%	0.36%	0.43%	0.45%	**0.47%**	0.34%	0.43%
HAUS-INVEST europa	0.44%	0.44%	0.38%	0.37%	0.35%	0.38%	0.33%	0.33%	**0.69%**	0.31%	0.33%	0.52%
SEB ImmoInvest	0.43%	0.47%	0.50%	0.39%	0.40%	0.46%	0.40%	0.44%	0.35%	0.49%	0.51%	**0.60%**
UniImmo: Deutschland	0.28%	0.38%	0.33%	0.39%	0.38%	0.35%	0.32%	**0.53%**	0.41%	0.38%	0.41%	0.35%
UniImmo: Europa	0.31%	0.36%	0.33%	0.40%	0.35%	0.41%	0.37%	0.37%	**0.54%**	0.37%	0.47%	0.34%
WestInvest 1	0.49%	0.31%	0.35%	0.35%	0.35%	0.28%	0.35%	0.38%	0.43%	0.14%	**0.54%**	0.35%

Figure 5.3 Mean monthly fund returns 1993-2008 by calendar month

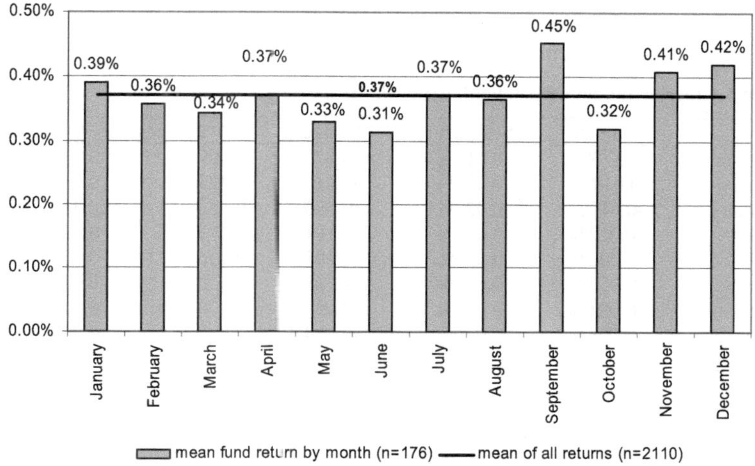

Following Hardin et al. (2005), we examine the month-of-the-year effect using the regression below with dummy variables representing the months of the year.

$$R_t = a_1 + a_2 Feb + ... + a_{12} Dec + e_t \qquad (5.2)$$

where R_t is the return in month t for the individual fund returns, Jan through Dec are the January to December dummy variables, and ε_t is a random error term. The intercept a_1 is the average return in April, which comes closest to the average return of all months and provides the benchmark. The coefficients a_2 to a_{12} compare the average return in April with the average returns of the other eleven months. The t-statistics for a_1 to a_{12} are adjusted for autocorrelation up to eight lags[62]. All estimates are made using OLS, applying the Newey-West (1987) autocorrelation consistent covariance matrix.

Table 5.4 shows that mean monthly returns differ significantly by calendar month. For September, the month to which most funds report to in their annual reports, returns are significantly higher at the 0.01 level, in December returns are higher as well, but significance only reaches the 0.1 level. In June and October, returns are significantly lower at the 0.1 level. Returns in March however do not differ significantly. The fact that funds which report to September also publish

62 We adjust for up to lag eight following Hardin et al. (2005). Adjustment up to lag twelve in the given context would impede the search for differences by calendar months.

accounting information at mid-year seems to have no significant impact on fund returns.

The non-parametric Wilcoxon Signed Rank Test confirms that the median returns in the mentioned months deviate from the median of all returns.

Table 5.4 Linear model with calendar months as dummy variables

	Estimate	Std. Error	t value	Pr(>|t|)	Sig.	WC	Sig.
(Intercept)	0.370%	0.015%	24.337	0.000	***	0.934	
January	0.019%	0.024%	0.802	0.423		0.065	*
February	-0.013%	0.022%	-0.596	0.552		0.336	
March	-0.027%	0.024%	-1.101	0.271		0.321	
May	-0.042%	0.020%	-2.103	0.036	**	0.004	***
June	-0.057%	0.024%	-2.328	0.020	**	0.018	**
July	-0.001%	0.022%	-0.038	0.970		0.892	
August	-0.006%	0.026%	-0.214	0.830		0.348	
September	0.082%	0.027%	3.033	0.002	***	0.005	***
October	-0.051%	0.029%	-1.777	0.076	*	0.098	*
November	0.037%	0.021%	1.762	0.078	*	0.038	**
December	0.050%	0.021%	2.379	0.017	**	0.002	***
F-statistic: 4.085 on 11 and 2098 DF, p-value: 0.0000058							

***, **, *, indicate statistical significance at the 0.01, 0.05 and 0.1 levels, respectively. The t-statistics are the Newey-West (1987) t-statistics adjusted for autocorrelation up to 8 lags. When using the automated lag selection of Newey-West (1994), significance levels do not change substantially. Without adjustment for autocorrelation, only September outperformance remains significant at the 0.01 level. Significance for June, October and December falls back to 0.1 levels. Wilcoxon Signed Rank Tests (for median values) confirm t-test results.

Table 5.5 shows the average ranking positions of the calendar months with respect to returns by fund. A low ranking position implies that many relatively high returns were realised in that particular month over the last 16 years. In case of CS EUROREAL, this means that the month December ranked on average over 16 years third (3.13) place, while February ranked 9th. The best average ranking position is indicated by bold figures and the month the funds report to is represented by grey shading of the cell. The ranking positions of EURIBOR and REXP returns are shown as well to account for liquidity performance, as funds invest part of their assets in cash and bond holdings. Results are fairly similar to mean return differences (Table 5.3), only the superiority of returns in September becomes even more evident, as September ranks on the best position for four out of eleven funds.

Figure 5.4 shows the number of ranking positions by month. If all ranking positions of monthly returns were evenly distributed over the year, one would expect that e.g. the month September realized 14.7 first rank positions from 1993 to 2008, 14.7 second rank positions and so on, since for each month (total: 176) and each fund (total: 11) one ranking position exists.

For the month September this means that out of 176 ranking positions realized in total, 34 were first rank and 20 were second rank.

Table 5.5 Average ranking positions of monthly returns

Fund	January	February	March	April	May	June	July	August	September	October	November	December
CS EUROREAL (A) EUR	6.38	9.06	6.31	6.50	6.31	4.56	6.94	8.81	6.00	8.44	5.56	**3.13**
DEGI EUROPA	**4.38**	6.94	5.88	7.00	6.81	8.38	5.50	8.13	7.69	6.31	6.13	4.88
Deka-ImmobilienFonds	5.38	6.25	6.94	6.25	8.38	6.69	**4.88**	6.63	5.69	6.50	7.44	6.88
EURO ImmoProfil	5.06	6.19	5.50	7.25	5.94	9.56	5.75	7.13	5.81	9.00	**4.50**	6.31
grundbesitz-europa	6.19	6.67	6.73	7.31	8.13	8.31	5.56	6.56	**4.38**	6.38	6.31	4.88
HANSAimmobilia	6.63	5.31	7.63	**4.56**	8.44	8.56	7.00	5.75	5.06	6.00	7.38	5.69
HAUS-INVEST europa	5.31	5.44	7.13	6.13	6.75	7.19	7.44	7.25	**3.75**	8.31	7.69	5.63
SEB ImmoInvest	7.19	7.00	5.94	7.88	7.56	6.38	7.38	5.94	8.31	5.69	5.19	**3.56**
UniImmo: Deutschland	7.13	6.31	7.44	5.63	7.31	6.69	7.50	6.06	**5.19**	6.38	5.50	6.88
UniImmo: Europa	6.38	6.75	7.25	6.69	7.31	6.25	6.88	6.31	**4.56**	6.88	5.31	7.44
WestInvest 1	4.44	7.13	6.44	6.75	6.38	8.13	6.94	5.88	5.56	9.63	**4.06**	6.69
all funds	5.76	6.63	6.67	6.60	7.15	7.24	6.47	6.71	**5.75**	7.13	5.87	5.75
EURIBOR	*5.06*	*5.94*	*6.19*	*5.88*	*6.50*	*6.19*	*6.25*	*7.00*	*6.75*	*6.81*	*6.50*	*6.31*
REXP	*5.44*	*7.19*	*7.38*	*8.00*	*7.19*	*7.25*	*6.06*	*5.75*	*6.00*	*6.44*	*4.75*	*6.56*

The lower ranks were realized less frequently than the expected value of 14.7 (= 176/12). The months with low mean returns May (0.33%) and October (0.32%) reached only ten respectively seven times the first rank within the respective years.

Figure 5.4 Ranking positions of September returns

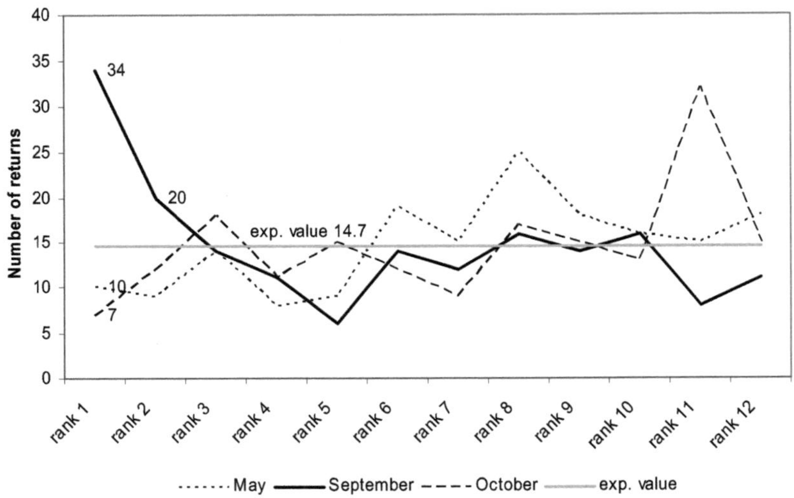

It can be concluded that mean monthly returns differ significantly by calendar month for the group of all eleven GOEFs. On the individual fund level given the limited number of only 16 observations for each month, return differences are significant only for some funds.

Table 5.6 shows that for DEGI EUROPA, Deka-ImmobilienFonds, and both funds of Union Investment, no significant return differences can be found. For the remaining seven funds however, at least in one month returns differ significantly (0.05 level) from the remaining returns of the respective fund. In case of CS EUROREAL and SEB ImmoInvest, returns are significantly higher in December, while grundbesitz-europa and HAUS-INVEST europa realize significantly higher returns in September. In June EURO ImmoProfil and HANSAimmobilia show significantly lower returns, and four other funds closely miss the 0.1 significance level. An interesting particularity is that SEB ImmoInvest returns differ weakly significant (p-value: 0.063) in September, but opposed to the majority of funds, the deviation is negative. As SEB ImmoInvest reports to March, this finding is not in contrast to the observed pattern that funds on average realise higher returns in the months they report to.

Trading Strategy

Given the fact that September returns are significantly higher in the case of HAUS-INVEST europa and significantly lower in the case of SEB ImmoInvest, we suggest a simple trading strategy: Invest in SEB ImmoInvest throughout the year (as the fund has achieved the highest mean returns over 16 years with the lowest volatility) with the exception of September. In September, shift the investment into HAUS-INVEST europa. With the exception of the years 2003 to 2005 where September returns of HAUS-INVEST europa were between 0.04 and 0.24 percentage points lower than SEB ImmoInvest's September returns, the remaining 13 September returns of HAUS-INVEST europa were between 0.02 and 1.31 percentage points higher than those of SEB ImmoInvest. On average, such a strategy would have resulted in 0.34 percentage points higher September returns between 1993 and 2008. As the returns of the other eleven months are not affected by the strategy, the annual return as well would have risen by 0.34 percentage points. In the presence of transaction costs via surcharge fees for private investors of 5% for most funds, the strategy seems more suitable for institutional investors, who face much lower surcharge fees. An alternative for private investors would be to trade participations via the secondary market (e.g. Fondsbörse Hamburg) where bid-ask spreads of funds like SEB ImmoInvest currently range around 0.10%. However, as the participation prices result from a market process and do not directly reflect net asset values, the question whether September return differences as well occur on the secondary market would have to be investigated.

We find no evidence that market participants apply the suggested trading strategy in an observable extent. When looking at monthly fund flows as percentage of fund volume, we find no evidence that the described strategy is being implemented. For those months with significantly deviating returns, either positive or negative, the fund flows do not differ significantly.

Regarding fund returns with twelve month time lag, we see that the three funds with correlation coefficients in excess of 0.3 also show significant return differences by calendar month. In case of SEB ImmoInvest, at least a part of the autocorrelation coefficient of 0.541 (Table 5.2) relates to significantly higher returns in December. For HAUS-INVEST europa, the significantly higher returns in September explain a part of the 0.397 coefficient of autocorrelation. In the case of EURO ImmoProfil, the significantly lower returns in June explain part of the serial correlation.

Figure 5.5 shows the distribution of all 2,110 monthly fund returns and exemplarily the distribution of the returns of the fund with the highest and at the same time least volatile mean returns (SEB ImmoInvest), the returns of EURO ImmoProfil, which have the lowest mean and the greatest standard deviation, and the returns of HAUS-INVEST europa, which exhibit the highest level of autocorrelation at lag twelve.

Table 5.6 Mann-Whitney U tests: Returns of individual months vs. all returns

Fund	January	February	March	April	May	June	July	August	September	October	November	December
CS EUROREAL (A) EUR	1.000	**0.044**	0.960	0.800	0.967	0.132	0.858	0.100	0.895	0.080	0.428	**0.005**
DEGI EUROPA	0.084	0.667	0.677	0.929	0.834	0.121	0.892	0.169	0.947	0.905	0.587	0.139
Deka-ImmobilienFonds	0.279	0.576	0.935	0.817	0.108	0.675	0.425	0.621	0.538	0.868	0.804	0.854
EURO ImmoProfil	0.281	0.667	0.851	0.731	0.881	**0.035**	0.570	0.670	0.405	0.121	0.291	0.909
grundbesitz-europa	0.894	0.701	0.489	0.542	0.085	0.109	0.508	0.785	**0.009**	0.805	0.696	0.090
HANSAimmobilia	0.858	0.391	0.256	0.142	**0.039**	**0.036**	0.774	0.507	0.391	0.356	0.638	0.269
HAUS-INVEST europa	0.334	0.325	0.664	0.864	0.496	0.410	0.403	0.272	**0.004**	0.179	0.413	0.170
SEB ImmoInvest	0.269	0.342	0.296	0.180	0.358	0.728	0.303	0.731	0.063	0.239	0.293	**0.001**
UniImmo: Deutschland	0.895	0.995	0.582	0.718	0.408	0.827	0.544	0.535	0.469	0.844	0.425	0.712
UniImmo: Europa	0.868	0.747	0.499	0.734	0.415	0.712	0.718	0.824	0.201	0.590	0.211	0.642
WestInvest 1	**0.019**	0.319	0.861	0.692	0.721	0.109	0.936	0.746	0.413	**0.025**	**0.027**	0.993

significance at 0.05 level indicated by bold figures

The return distribution of all funds together is quite symmetrical, with a skewness of -0.315. It is not normal though, as it is sharply peaked around the mean with an excess kurtosis of 16.121. The characteristic of leptokurtic returns is true for all GOEFs, but skewness parameters differ. In the presented examples, SEB ImmoInvest has a positive skewness of 1.439, while the return structure of EURO ImmoProfil has a negative skewness of -3.972. HAUS-INVEST europa has a return distribution that is positively skewed (skewness: 1.287) due to fat a fat tail at the right side. This fat tail consists basically out of six returns in excess of 1.0% per month and four out of them fall into September.

For all funds, 43 returns out of 2,110 are in excess of 1.0% and 13 of these fall into September. For the 43 most negative returns which are below -0.14%, only six were realised in September, but 17 in June and twelve in October. Among the highest third of SEB ImmoInvest fund returns (59 out of 176) in contrast, no single return falls into September, while all other months are represented at least three times within those 59 returns. A possible explanation for not showing high returns in September when the majority of competitors do so might be the fact that the correlation of the fund's return to the market of the open-end funds (e.g. measured by the OFIX index) becomes smaller this way. A low correlation to the market results in high values of beta-based performance measures such as the Treynor Ratio. Research like the IPD open-end funds study or Thomas et al. (2009) calculate those performance measures and rank funds accordingly.

5.5 Conclusion

We see no indication why the property performance that is directly reflected in property fund returns should be generally higher in September. We rather argue that timing of valuations or influence on valuers result in the described persistent return differences by calendar month. In case of the month September, the fact that many funds report to that date might be an incentive for fund management to improve year-on-year fund performance and thus increase performance-based compensation.

A second result is that autocorrelation of German open-end fund returns cannot be solely attributed to the appraisal process, as an appraisal frequency of twelve months would not explain significantly higher returns (September), or significantly lower returns (June) over a period of 16 years. If a big proportion of appraisals fell into one single month, this would explain higher return defections in that month, but this cannot be observed in the standard errors of fund returns (Table 5.4). Biases upwards or downwards however cannot be attributed to the valuation frequency.

If we follow the argumentation that funds have the possibility to shift returns between months in order to show for example higher returns in September, it also seems possible for funds like SEB ImmoInvest that managers use the knowledge of significantly higher returns in September of their competitors to present low returns in that month with the aim to improve beta-based performance measures, particularly as SEB ImmoInvest reports to March. Although this is presumptive evidence, it would explain why SEB ImmoInvest is the only fund that shows the lowest mean returns (Table 5.3) and the lowest ranking position of returns (Table 5.5) in September, while the returns of the competitors as a group are significantly higher in that month (Table 5.4).

The results contribute to previous research on autocorrelation of fund returns in that respective that autocorrelation is examined on individual fund level as contrasted to autocorrelation on aggregated index level. As there is evidence at least for some funds that the return structure is influenced by the reporting period and given the fact that the reporting periods differs among funds, autocorrelation should be investigated on individual fund level rather than on index level.

Figure 5.5 Histogram of monthly fund returns 1993-2008

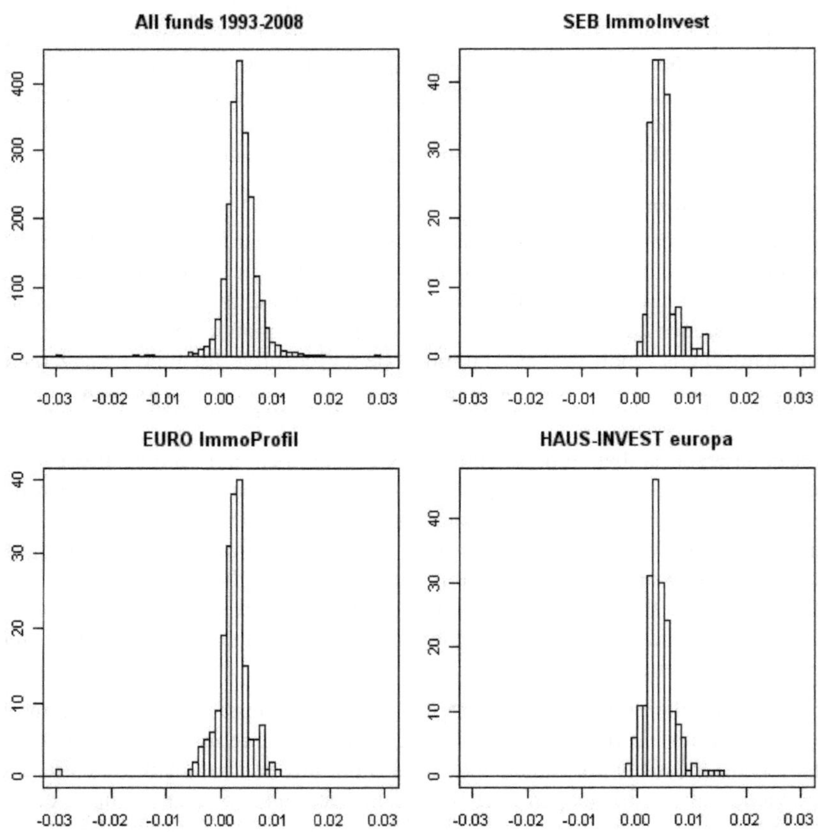

6 Conclusion

The analysis of the distribution of appraisals of German open-end fund's German properties (chapter 2) has shown that in fund crisis year 2006 there have been significant differences of property valuation between funds' portfolios. The arguably most likely explanation for different mean value changes of properties by portfolio is that funds exerted an influence on the valuation of their properties in the year 2006. Only those variables differ significantly in 2006 compared to 2005 and 2007 that are derived within the valuation process such as the change in market value, the change in rental value and the change in the year's purchase. In contrast, the variables occupancy rate, change in occupancy rate and the percentage of ending leases, which are central input factors within the valuation process, do not change noticeably in 2006. This is further evidence that the valuation results were different in 2006 but not the relevant market developments.

The valuation results of GOEF properties in all the investigated foreign markets Belgium, France, Italy, the Netherlands, Spain and the UK (chapter 3) differ significantly from the valuations of the local market participants in the respective markets. Especially when comparing GOEFs UK capital growth rates from Q1 2005 to Q1 2008 to IPD UK capital growth, a substantial smoothing effect is found. While the change in rental values is at least similar within GOEFs compared to IPD figures, the yield shift differs extremely. German open-end funds do not change the capitalization rates of their foreign investments in a comparable way to the local market participants. A further and unexpected valuation patter was found: The negative relation between the rental value change and the rent multiplier, with the consequence of smoother property value changes than the volatility of the rental value would suggest. The negative correlation of the rental value change and the change of the rent multiplier has the effect that changes in rental values are not fully reflected in changes of the market values, which again partly explains smoothed value changes of properties held by German open-end funds.

Chapter 4 presents a strong indication for timing effects of property valuations on the variance of monthly fund returns. The expected link between asset concentration and fund return variance does not hold empirically. For most funds, high value changes of single properties did not result in extreme return deflections in the respective months. The existence of valuation timing by the fund management with the effect of smoothing monthly fund returns is problematic for several reasons. As most performance benchmarks are based on a mean/ variance framework, return smoothing decreases fund return variance and thus improves the ranking position of the respective fund. In multi asset portfolio optimisation applications, smoothed returns can result in an over allocation of the respective asset to the disadvantage of the investor.

Results of chapter 5 show persistent return differences by calendar month. In case of the month September, the fact that many funds report to that date might be an incentive for fund management to improve year-based fund performance and thus increase performance-based compensation. A second result is that autocorrelation of German open-end fund returns cannot be solely attributed to the appraisal process, as an appraisal frequency of twelve months would not explain significantly higher returns (September), or significantly lower returns (June) over a period of 16 years. The results contribute to previous research on autocorrelation of fund returns in that respective that autocorrelation is examined on individual fund level as contrasted to autocorrelation on aggregated index level. As there is evidence at least for some funds that the return structure is influenced by the reporting period and given the fact that the reporting periods differs among funds, autocorrelation should be investigated on individual fund level rather than on index level.

Multiple-smoothed returns and consequences on portfolio optimisation

All four presented essays show evidence on smoothed and / or biased returns, either on the property level (essays 1 and 2) or on the fund level (essays 3 and 4). As the sources of return smoothing are different from those addressed by previous research, classical approaches to derive true real estate volatility from appraisal-based time series are not applicable. The impression that fund management is actively involved in smoothing monthly fund returns aggravates the problem. Results show three different pieces of evidence on return smoothing, namely via the influence on valuation (essay 1 and 2), via the timing of valuations (essay 3) and via influence on returns resulting in return differences by calendar months. Together with the notion of internationally uniquely stable returns, it seems not possible to extract true asset volatility from the observed appraisal-based time series. It is not possible to evaluate the true investment risk from the historical return series of GOEFs as it is the case for stock and bond investments, because in the case of redemption stops and the subsequent sale of properties at true market values, the fund returns instantly reflect the so far incorrectly incorporated developments on the property market. This ascertainment calls urgently for research on how to evaluate investment risk of GOEFs. Using returns that are being smoothed in multiple ways with the consequence of artificially low volatilities in portfolio optimisation procedures leads to invalid results that overestimated portfolio weights of GOEFs.

Persistent appraisal problems despite high levels of transparency

Research and market participants frequently demand a higher transparency within the real estate market to better describe and analyse the risk and return characteristics of the illiquid asset class real estate. The results of the four presented essays however show that transparency is not an end in itself. For GOEFs, all monthly returns are available, and from 2006 onwards all individual property values are available as well. Severe smoothing and return deferring patterns could be shown with limited statistical efforts nevertheless. The shortcoming with respect to the highly regulated and thus transparent asset class of open-end real estate funds in Germany is therefore not a lack of transparency, but rather indifference from market participants and regulatory bodies with respect to the evident problems in the fields of appraisal and return smoothing. In the light of recent redemption stops of fund participations of major GOEFs and the unprecedented negative monthly return of -13.9% in July 2009 of the fund Morgan Stanley P2 Value as a consequence of massive property devaluations, the described return and appraisal anomalies seem unacceptable from an investor protection point of view. Both fund management and appraisers have to address those issues or the supervisory authorities need to assume responsibility.

References

Abraham, A., & Ikenberry, D.L. (1994). The individual investor and the weekend effect. *Journal of Financial and Quantitative Analysis 29*(2), 263-277.

Adair, A., Berry, J., & McGreal, S. (1996). Valuation of residential property: Analysis of participant behaviour. *Journal of Property Valuation and Investment, 14*(1), 20-35.

Amidu, A., & Aluko, B.T. (2007). Client influence on valuation: Perceptual analysis of the driving factors. *International Journal of Strategic Property Management, 11*(2), 77-89.

Amidu, A., Aluko, B.T., & Hansz, J.A. (2008). Client feedback pressure and the role of estate surveyors and valuers. *Journal of Property Research, 25*(2), 89-106.

Bannier, C.E., Fecht, F., & Tyrell, M. (2008). Open-end real estate funds in Germany: Genesis and crisis. *Kredit und Kapital, 41*(1), 9-36.

Barkham, R., Geltner, D. (1994). Unsmoothing British valuation-based returns without assuming an efficient market. *Journal of Property Research, 11*(2), 81-95.

Baroni, M., Barthélémy, F., & Mokrane, M. (2007). Using rents and price dynamics in real estate portfolio valuation. *Property Management, 25*(5), 462-486.

Benk, K., Haß, L.H., Johanning, L., & Rudolph, B. (Eds.). (2008). *Offene Immobilienfonds als wesentlicher Baustein einer erfolgreichen Asset Allocation.* Vallendar, Germany: WHU - Otto Beisheim School of Management, Lehrstuhl für empirische Kapitalmarktforschung.

Black, R. (1997). Expert property negotiators and pricing information. Revisited. *Journal of Property Valuation and Investment, 15*(3), 274-281.

Black, R., & Diaz, J. (1996). The use of information versus asking price in the real property negotiation process. *Journal of Property Research, 13*(2), 287-297.

Bond, S., & Hwang, S. (2003). A measure of fundamental volatility in the commercial property market. *Real Estate Economics, 31*(4), 577-600.

Bretten, G.R., & Whyatt, P. (2002). Variance in property valuations for commercial lending. *RICS Research Papers, 4*(9), 1-16.

Brounen, D., & Eichholtz, P. (2003). Property, common stock, and property shares. *Journal of Portfolio Management, 30*(special issue on real estate), 129-137.

Brounen, D., Op 't Veld, H., & Raitio, V. (2007). Transparency in the European non-listed real estate funds market. *Journal of Real Estate Portfolio Management, 13*(2), 107-117.

Brounen, D., & ter Laak, M. (2005). Understanding the discount: Evidence from European property shares. *Journal of Real Estate Portfolio Management, 11*(3), 241-251.

Brown, G.R. (1991). Property investment and the capital markets. London: E & FN Spon.

Brueggemann, W.B., Chen, A.H., & Thibodeau, T.G. (1992). Some additional evidence on the performance of commingled real estate investment funds: 1972-1991. *Journal of Real Estate Research, 7*(4), 433-449.

Bundesverband Investment und Assetmanagement (2009a). Offene Immobilienfonds haben ausgewogene Portfoliostruktur. Press release, 02-04-2009, Frankfurt: Author.

Bundesverband Investment und Assetmanagement (2009b). Positive Entscheidungen zur Anlage von Mündelgeldern Offene Immobilienfonds. Press release, 03-02-2009, Frankfurt: Author.

Byrne, P., & Lee, S. (1997). Real estate portfolio analysis under conditions of non-normality: The case of NCREIF. *Journal of Real Estate Portfolio Management, 3*(1), 37-46.

Chan, S.H., Leung, W.K., & Wang, K. (2005). Changes in REIT structure and stock performance: Evidence from the Monday stock anomaly. *Real Estate Economics 33*(1), 89-120.

Chen, Y.C., & Yu, S.M. (2009). Client influence on valuation: Does language matter? *Journal of Property Investment & Finance, 27*(1), 25-41.

Chiang, Y.H., So, J.C.K., & Yeung, S.C.W. (2006). Real option premium in Hong Kong land prices. *Journal of Property Investment and Finance, 24*(3), 239-258.

Chinloy, P., Cho, M., & Megbolugbe, I. (1997). Appraisals, transaction incentives, and smoothing. *Journal of Real Estate Finance and Economics, 14*(1/2), 89-112.

Cho, H., Kawaguchi, Y., & Shilling, J. (2003). Unsmoothing commercial property returns: A revision to Fisher-Geltner-Webb's unsmoothing. *Journal of Real Estate Finance and Economics*, *27*(3), 393-405.

Clayton, J., Geltner, D., & Hamilton, S.W. (2001). Smoothing in commercial property valuations: Evidence from individual appraisals. *Real Estate Economics, 29*(3), 337-361.

Conover, C.M., Friday, S.H., & Sirmans, G.S. (2002). Diversification benefits from foreign real estate investments. *Journal of Real Estate Portfolio Management, 8*(1), 17-25.

Corgel, J., & deRoss, J. (1999). Recovery of real estate returns for portfolio allocations. *Journal of Real Estate Finance and Economics, 18*(3), 279-296.

Crosby, N. (2007). German open ended funds: Was there a valuation problem? Retrieved May 20, 2009, from University of Reading, Web site: www.reading.ac.uk/REP/wp/wp0507.html.

Crosby, N., Devaney, S., & Murray, C. (2009a). Measuring depreciation in European office markets - Just another valuation problem? Paper presented at the European Real Estate Society conference, Stockholm, Sweden.

Crosby, N., Lizieri, C., & McAllister, P. (2009b). Means, motive and opportunity? Disentangling client influence on performance measurement appraisals. Paper presented at the European Real Estate Society conference, Stockholm, Sweden.

Cypher, M.L., & Hansz, J.A. (2003). Does assessed value influence market value judgments? *Journal of Property Research, 20*(4), 305-308.

D'Agostino, R.B., Belanger, A., & D'Agostino, R.B.Jr. (1990). A suggestion for using powerful and informative tests of normality. *The American Statistician, 44*(4), 16-32.

De Wit, D.P.M. (1993). Smoothing bias in in-house appraisal-based returns of open-end real estate funds. *Journal of Real Estate Research, 8*(2), 157-170.

Diaz, J. (1990). How appraisers do their work: A test of the appraisal process and the development of a descriptive model. *Journal of Real Estate Research, 5*(1), 1-16.

Diaz, J. (1997). An investigation into the impact of previous expert value estimates on appraisal judgment. *Journal of Real Estate Research, 13*(1), 57-66.

Diaz, J., & Hansz, J.A. (1997). How valuers use the value opinion of others. *Journal of Property Valuation and Investment, 15*(3), 256-260.

Diaz, J., & Hansz, J.A. (2001). The use of reference points in valuation judgment. *Journal of Property Research, 18*(2), 141-148.

Diaz, J., Gallimore, P., & Levy, D. (2002). Residential valuation behaviour in the United States, the United Kingdom and New Zealand. *Journal of Property Research, 19*(4), 313-326.

Diaz, J., & Wolverton, M.L. (1998). A longitudinal examination of the appraisal smoothing hypothesis. *Real Estate Economics, 26*(2), 349-358.

Diaz, J., Zhao, R., & Black, R. (1999). Does contingent reward reduce negotiation anchoring? *Journal of Property Investment and Finance, 17*(4), 374-379.

Domrow, J., & Turnbull, G.K. (2004). Trends in real estate research, 1988-2001: What's hot and what's not? *Journal of Real Estate Finance and Economics, 29*(1), 47-70.

Downie, M.L., Schulte, K-W., & Thomas, M. (1996). Germany. In Adair, A., Downie, ML, McGreal, S., & Vos, G. (Ed), European valuation practice. London: E & FN Spon.

Efron, B., & Tibshirani, R.J. (1993). *An introduction to the bootstrap*. New York: Chapman & Hall/CRC.

Fama, E., & Jensen, M. (1983). Agency problems and residual claims. *Journal of Law and Economics, 26*(2), 327-349.

Farncombe, M., & Waller, A. (2007). Using simulation to optimise renting and space planning decisions. *Journal of Corporate Real Estate*, *9*(3), 156-167.

Fingleton, B. (2008). A generalized method of moments estimator for a spatial model with moving average errors, with application to real estate prices. *Empirical Economics*, *34*(1), 35-57.

Fisher, D.F., Geltner, D., & Webb, R.B. (1994). Value indices of commercial real estate: A comparison of index construction methods. *Real Estate Finance, 16*(3), 9-15.

Fisher, D.F., Geltner, D., & Webb, R.B. (1999). How reliable are commercial property appraisals? *Journal of Real Estate Finance and Economics, 9*(2), 137-164.

Ferguson, J.T. (1988). After-sale evaluations: Appraisals or justifications. *The Journal of Real Estate Research, 3*(1), 19-26.

Firoozi, F., Hollas, D.R., Rutherford, R.C., & Thomson, T.A. (2006). Property assessment and information asymmetry in residential real estate. *Journal of Real Estate Research. 28*(3), 275-291.

Friday, H.S., & Higgins, E.J. (2000). The day of the week effect in real estate investment trusts. *Journal of Real Estate Portfolio Management, 6*(3), 273-282.

Friday, H.S., & Peterson, D.R. (1997). January return seasonality in real estate investment trusts: Information vs. tax-loss selling effects. *Journal of Financial Research, 20*(1), 33-51.

Gallo, J.G., Lockwood, L.J., & Rodriguez, M. (2006). Differentiating CREF performance. *Real Estate Economics, 34*(2), 173-209.

Gallimore, P. (1994). Aspects of information processing in valuation judgment and choice. *Journal of Property Research, 11*(2), 97-110.

Gallimore, P. (1996). Confirmation bias in the valuation process: A test for corroborating evidence. *Journal of Property Research, 13*(4), 261-273.

Gallimore, P., & Gray, A. (2002). The role of investor sentiment in property investment decisions. *Journal of Property Research, 19*(2), 111-120.

Gallimore, P., Hansz, J., & Gray, A. (2000). Decision making in small property companies. *Journal of Property Investment and Finance, 18*(6), 602-612.

Gallimore, P., & Wolverton, M.L. (1997). Price knowledge induced bias: A cross cultural comparison. *Journal of Property Valuation and Investment, 15*(3), 261-273.

Gallimore, P., & Wolverton, M.L. (2000). The objective in valuation: A study of the influence of client feedback. *Journal of Property Research, 17*(1), 47-58.

Geltner, D. (1989a). Bias in appraisal-based returns. *Journal of the American Real Estate and Urban Economics Association, 17*(3), 338-352.

Geltner, D. (1989b). Estimating real estate's systematic risk from aggregate level appraisal-based returns. *Real Estate Economics, 17*(4), 463-481.

Geltner, D. (1991). Smoothing in appraisal-based returns. *Journal of Real Estate Finance and Economics, 4*(3), 327-345.

Geltner, D. (1993). Estimating market values from appraised values without assuming an efficient market. *Journal of Real Estate Research, 8*(3), 325-345.

Geltner, D. (1993). Temporary aggregation in real estate return indices. *Journal of the American Real Estate and Urban Economics Association, 21*(2), 141-166.

Geltner, D. (1998). Appraisal smoothing: The other side of the story - a comment. Financial Economic Network at: http://www.ssrn.com. Working Paper, Department of Finance, University of Cincinnati.

Geltner, D., MacGregor, B.D., & Schwann, G.M. (2003). Appraisal smoothing and price discovery in real estate markets. *Urban Studies, 40*(5), 1047-1064.

Getmansky, M., Lo, A., & Makarov, I. (2004). An econometric model of serial correlation and illiquidity in hedge fund returns. *Journal of Financial Economics, 74*(3), 529-609.

Giaccotto, C., & Clapp, J. (1992). Appraisal-based real estate returns under alternative market regimes. *Journal of the American Real Estate and Urban Economics Association, 20*(1), 1-24.

Gordon, J., Canter, T.A., & Webb, J.R. (1998). The effect of international real estate securities on portfolio diversification. *Journal of Real Estate Portfolio Management, 4*(2), 83-91.

Graff, R.A., Harrington, A., & Young, M.S. (1997). The shape of Australian real estate return distributions and comparisons to the United States. *Journal of Real Estate Research, 14*(3), 291-308.

Graff, R.A., & Young, M.S. (1999). The magnitude of random appraisal error in commercial real estate valuation. *Journal of Real Estate Research, 17*(1/2), 33-54.

Hamilton, S.W., & Clayton, J. (1999). Smoothing in commercial property valuations: Evidence from the trenches. *Real Estate Finance, 16*(3), 16-26.

Hansz, J.A., & Diaz, J. (2001). Valuation bias in commercial appraisal: A transaction price feedback experiment. *Real Estate Economics, 29*(4), 553-565.

Hardin, W.G., Liano, K., & Huang, G-C. (2005). Real estate investment trusts and calendar anomalies: Revisited. *International Real Estate Review, 8*(1), 83-94.

Havard, T.M. (1999). Do valuers have a greater tendency to adjust a previous valuation upwards or downwards? *Journal of Property Investment & Finance, 17*(4), 365-373.

Havard, T.M. (2001). An experimental evaluation of the effect of data presentation on heuristics bias in commercial valuation. *Journal of Property Research, 18*(1), 51-68.

Heckman, J.J. (1979). Sample selection bias as a specification error. *Econometrica, 47*(1), 153-161.

Hendershott, P.H., & Kane, E.J. (1995). U.S. office market values during the past decade: How distorted have appraisals been? *Real Estate Economics, 23*(2), 101-116.

Hoesli, M., & Hamelink, F. (1996). Diversification of Swiss portfolios with real estate. *Journal of Property Valuation and Investment, 14*(5), 59-75.

Hoesli, M., Jani, E., & Bender, A. (2006). Monte Carlo simulations for real estate valuation. *Journal of Property Investment & Finance, 24*(2), 102-122.

Hordijk, A.C., de Kroon, H.M., & Theebe, M.A. (2004). Long-run return series for the European continent: 25 years of Dutch commercial real estate. *Journal of Real Estate Portfolio Management, 10*(3), 217-230.

Ibbotson, R., & Siegel, L. (1984). Real estate returns: A comparison with other investments. *Journal of the American Real Estate and Urban Economics Association, 12*(3), 219-241.

Investment Act (2008) 2003-12-15 (BGBl. I p. 2676). as amended on 2008-08-13 (BGBl. I p. 1690).

IPD. (2008). *IPD index guide* - (4th ed.). London: Author.

IPD. (2009a). *IPD UK quarterly digest Q1 2009*. London: Author.

IPD. (2009b). *IPD multi national index spreadsheet 2008 - update 4*. London: Author.

IPD Investment Property Databank GmbH. (2007). Erläuterungen zum Datenerhebungsblatt. Wiesbaden, Germany: Author.

IPD Investment Property Databank GmbH. (2008). *Performance-Studie Offene Immobilienfonds 2008*. Wiesbaden, Germany: Author.

IPD Investment Property Databank GmbH. (2009a). *Performance-Studie Offene Immobilienfonds 2009*. Wiesbaden, Germany: Author.

IPD Investment Property Databank GmbH. (2009b). *German digest*. Wiesbaden, Germany: Author.

IPD Investment Property Databank GmbH. (2009c). *IPD German open ended funds index Q1 2009*. Wiesbaden, Germany: Author.

Keim, D., & Stambaugh, R. (1984). A further investigation of the weekend effect in stock returns. *Journal of Finance 30*(3), 819-884.

Kinnard, W.N., Lenk, M.M., & Worzala, E.M. (1997). Client pressure in the commercial appraisal industry: How prevalent is it? *Journal of Property Valuation and Investment 15*(3), 233-244.

Koenker, R.W., & Basset, G.Jr. (1978). Regression quantiles. *Econometrica 46*(1), 33-50.

Koenker, R.W., & Hallock, K.F. (2001). Quantile regressi*on. Journal of Economic Perspectives, 15*(4), 143-156.

Kurzrock, B., Gläsner, S., & Wilke, E. (2009). Performance of open-end real estate funds in Germany: Are institutional investors better off than retail investors? *Journal of European Property Research, 2*(2), 110-131.

Kurzrock, B., Rottke, N.B., & Schiereck, D. (2009). Factors that influence the performance of office properties. *Journal of Real Estate Portfolio Management, 15*(1), 59-73.

Lai, T.-Y., & Wang, K. (1998). Appraisal smoothing: The other side of the story. *Real Estate Economics, 26*(3), 511-535.

Lee, M-L., & Lee, M-T. (2003). Institutional involvement and the REIT January effect over time. *Journal of Property Investment & Finance, 21*(6), 435-449.

Levy, D., & Schuck, E.J. (1999). The influence of clients on valuations. *Journal of Property Investment & Finance, 17*(4), 380-400.

Levy, D., & Schuck, E.J. (2005). The influence of clients on valuations: The clients' perspective. *Journal of Property Investment & Finance, 23*(2), 182-201.

Lunneborg, C.E. (2000). Data analysis by resampling: Concepts and applications. University of Michigan: Duxbury Press.

MacFarland, J., Pettit, R., & Sung, S. (1982). The distribution of foreign exchange price changes: Trading day effects and risk measurement. *Journal of Finance 37*(3), 693-715.

MacGregor, B.D., & Nanthakumaran, N. (1992). The allocation to property in the multiasset portfolio: The evidence and theory reconsidered. *Journal of Property Research, 9*(1), 5-32.

McParland, C., Adair, A., & McGreal, S. (2002). Valuation standards: A comparison of four European countries. *Journal of Property Investment and Finance, 20*(2), 127-141.

Manly, B.F.J. (2007). *Randomization, bootstrap and Monte Carlo methods in biology* (3rd ed.). Boca Raton, FL: Chapman & Hall/CRC.

Maurer, R., Reiner, F., & Sebastian, S. (2004). Characteristics of German real estate return distributions: Evidence from Germany and comparison to the U.S. and U.K. *Journal of Real Estate Portfolio Management, 10*(1), 59-76.

Maurer, R., & Sebastian, S. (2002). Inflation risk analysis of European real estate securities. *Journal of Real Estate Research, 24*(1), 47-77.

Miles, M., Cole, R., & Guilkey, D. (1990). A different look at commercial real estate returns. *Journal of the American Real Estate and Urban Economics Association, 18*(4), 403-430.

Mueller, G.R., Boney, V., & Mueller, A.G. (2008). International real estate volatility: A tactical investment strategy. *Journal of Real Estate Portfolio Management, 14*(4), 415-423.

Myer, F.C.N., & Webb, J.R. (1994). Statistical properties of returns: Financial assets versus commercial real estate. *Journal of Real Estate Finance and Economics, 8*(3), 267-282.

Newell, G., & MacFarlane, J. (1996). Risk estimation and appraisal-smoothing in UK property returns. *Journal of Property Research, 13*(1), 1-12.

Newey, W.K., & West, K.D. (1987). A simple, positive semi-definite, heteroscedasticity and autocorrelation consistent covariance matrix. *Econometrica, 55*(3), 703-708.

Newey, W.K., & West, K.D. (1994). Automatic lag selection in covariance matrix estimation. *The Review of Economic Studies, 61*(4), 631-653.

Northcraft, G.B., & Neale, M.A. (1987). Experts, amateurs and real estate: An anchoring and adjustment perspective on property pricing decisions. *Organisational Behaviour and Human Decision Processes, 39*(1), 84-97.

Patel, K., Paxson, D., & Sing, T.S. (2005). A review of the practical uses of real property options. *RICS Research Paper Series, 5*(1), 1-19.

Quan, D.C., & Quigley, J.M. (1991). Price formation and the appraisal function in real estate markets. *Journal of Real Estate Finance and Economics, 4*(2), 127-146.

Quigg, L. (1993). Empirical testing of real option-pricing models. *Journal of Finance, 48*(2), 621-640.

Redman, A.L., Manakyan, H., & Liano, K. (1997). Real estate investment trusts and calendar anomalies. *Journal of Real Estate Research, 14*(1/2), 19-28.

Rodgers, J.L. (1999). The bootstrap, the jackknife, and the randomization test: A sample taxonomy. *Multivariate Behavioral Research, 34*(4), 411-456.

Rushmore, S. (1993). Ethics in hotel appraising. *Appraisal Journal, 61*(3), 357-363.

Shimizu, C., & Nishimura, K.G. (2006). Biases in appraisal land price information: The case of Japan. *Journal of Property Investment and Finance, 24*(2), 150-175.

Sing, T.F. (2001). Optimal timing of a real estate development under uncertainty. *Journal of Property Investment and Finance, 19*(1), 35-52.

Smith, H.C. (1986). Inconsistencies in appraisal theory and practice. *The Journal of Real Estate Research, 1*(1), 1-17.

Smolen, G.E. (1994). Do we need a statewide appraisal peer review system? *The Appraisal Journal, 62*(1), 86-93.

Smolen, G.E., & Hambleton, D.C. (1997). Is the real estate appraiser's role too much to expect? *The Appraisal Journal, 65*(1), 9-17.

Spence, M.T., & Thorson, J. (1998). The effect of expertise on the quality of appraisal services. *Journal of Real Estate Research, 15*(1/2), 205-215.

Stevenson, S. (2000). Momentum effects and mean reversion in real estate securities. *Journal of Real Estate Research, 23*(1/2), 47-65.

Tang, B.S., Yiu, C.Y., Chiang, Y.H., & Choy, L.H.T. (2006). A three-dimensional model of land appraisal. Unpublished discussion paper. Department of Building and Real Estate, The Hong Kong Polytechnic University.

Thomas, M. (1997). Die Entwicklung eines Performanceindexes für den deutschen Immobilienmarkt. Köln: Müller.

Thomas, M., Piazolo, D., & Gläsner, S.M. (2009). *Analyzing the changing risk and return structure of German open-ended funds using semivariance based performance measures*. Paper presented at the American Real Estate Society Conference, Monterey, USA.

Titman, S. (1985). Urban land prices under uncertainty. *American Economic Review, 75*(3), 505-514.

Wang, K., Li, Y., & Erickson, J. (1997). A new look at the Monday effect. *Journal of Finance 52*(5), 2171-2186.

Wang, P. (2006). Errors in variables, links between variables and recovery of volatility information in appraisal-based real estate return indexes. *Real Estate Economics, 34*(4), 497-518.

Webb, R.B. (1994). On the reliability of commercial appraisals: An analysis of properties sold from the Russel-NCREIF Index (1978-1992). *Real Estate Finance, 11*(1), 62-65.

White, H. (1980). A heteroscedasticity-consistent covariance matrix estimator and a direct test for heteroscedasticity. *Econometrica, 48*(4), 817-838.

Williams, J.T. (1991). Real estate development as an option. *Journal of Real Estate Finance and Economics, 4*(2), 191-208.

Wofford, L. (1978). A simulation approach to the appraisal of income producing real estate. *Journal of the American Real Estate & Urban Economics Association, 6*(4), 370-394.

Wolverton, M.L. (2000). Self-perception of the role of the appraiser: Objective opinions or price validation. *The Appraisal Journal, 68*(3), 272-282.

Wolverton, M.L., & Gallimore, P. (1999). Client feedback and the role of the appraiser. *Journal of Real Estate Research, 18*(3), 415-432.

Worzala, E.M., Lenk, M.M., & Kinnard, W.N. (1998). How client pressure affects the appraisal of residential property. *The Appraisal Journal, 66*(4), 416-427.

Yamazaki, R. (2001). Empirical testing of real option pricing models using land price index in Japan. *Journal of Property Investment and Finance, 19*(1), 53-72.

Yiu, C.J., Tang, B.S., Chiang, Y.H., & Choy, L.H.T. (2006). Alternative theories of appraisal bias. *Journal of Real Estate Literature, 14*(3), 321-344.

Young, M.S. (2005). Making sense of the NCREIF property index: A new formulation revisited. *Journal of Real Estate Portfolio Management, 11*(3), 211-223.

Young, M.S. (2008). Revisiting non-normal real estate return distributions by property type in the U.S. *Journal of Real Estate Finance and Economics, 36*(2), 233-248.

Young, M.S., & Graff, R.A. (1995). Real estate is not normal: A fresh look at real estate return distributions. *Journal of Real Estate Finance and Economics, 10*(3), 225-259.

Young, M.S., Lee, S.L., & Devaney, S.P. (2006). Non-normal real estate return distributions by property type in the UK. *Journal of Property Research, 23*(2), 109-133.

Declaration of Honor

I declare upon my word of honor that the dissertation submitted herewith is entirely my own work and that only the sources and aids listed have been used. All references or quotations in any form and their use have been clearly identified in the source references.

Sebastian Michael Gläsner

Wiesbaden, September 14, 2009

Corporate Finance and Governance

Herausgegeben von Dirk Schiereck

Band 1 Sebastian Michael Gläsner: Return Patterns of German Open-End Real Estate Funds. An Empirical Explanation of Smooth Fund Returns. 2010.

Band 2 Patrick Ams: Directors' Dealings and Insider Trading in Germany. An Empirical Analysis. 2010.

www.peterlang.de